CAMBRIDGE MUSIC HANDBOOKS

Mahler: *Das Lied von der Erde*

Since its premiere Mahler's *Das Lied von der Erde* ("The Song of the Earth") has been widely regarded as his finest masterpiece – "the most Mahleresque of his works," according to his friend and disciple, the conductor Bruno Walter. And as Mahler himself wrote to Walter when the draft score was finished, "I believe it is the most personal thing I have yet created." *Das Lied* was written in the wake of three catastrophic events that shook the foundations of Mahler's life in 1907, and like all his earlier works, it is deeply influenced by the composer's personal and philosophical worldview. The opening chapter, "Background: Mahler's 'symphonic worlds' before 1908," sets the stage for a study of the work's genesis, a summary of the most important critiques of the premiere, and a careful reading of this six-movement symphony for voices and orchestra.

An appendix provides an interlinear translation that makes Mahler's superb treatment of texts accessible to readers with little or no knowledge of German.

STEPHEN E. HEFLING is Associate Professor at Case Western Reserve University. He is editor of *Mahler Studies* (Cambridge, 1997) as well as *Nineteenth-Century Chamber Music* (New York, 1998), and has edited *Das Lied von der Erde* for the Mahler Kritische Gesamtausgabe (Vienna, 1989).

CAMBRIDGE MUSIC HANDBOOKS

GENERAL EDITOR Julian Rushton

Mahler: *Das Lied von der Erde*
(*The Song of the Earth*)

Stephen E. Hefling

CAMBRIDGE
UNIVERSITY PRESS

CAMBRIDGE UNIVERSITY PRESS
Cambridge, New York, Melbourne, Madrid, Cape Town, Singapore, São Paulo

Cambridge University Press
The Edinburgh Building, Cambridge CB2 2RU, UK

Published in the United States of America by Cambridge University Press, New York

www.cambridge.org
Information on this title: www.cambridge.org/9780521475341

First published 2000

A catalogue record for this publication is available from the British Library

Library of Congress Cataloguing in Publication data

Hefling, Stephen E.
Mahler, Das Lied von der Erde = (The song of the earth) / Stephen E. Hefling
p.   cm. – (Cambridge music handbooks)
Includes bibliographical references and index.
ISBN 0 521 47534 1 (hardback) – ISBN 0 521 47558 9 (paperback)
1. Mahler, Gustav, 1860–1911. Lied von der Erde.   I. Title.
II. Title: Lied von der Erde.   III. Title: Song of the earth.
IV. Series.
MT121.M34H44   1999
782.4′7–dc21   99-23189   CIP

ISBN-13 978-0-521-47534-1 hardback
ISBN-10 0-521-47534-1 hardback

ISBN-13 978-0-521-47558-7 paperback
ISBN-10 0-521-47558-9 paperback

Transferred to digital printing 2005

Noch ein Buch für Deborah!

Contents

Illustrations

Preface

Since its premiere in 1911, six months after the composer's death, *Das Lied von der Erde* has been widely regarded as Mahler's finest masterpiece – "the most 'Mahleresque' of his works" according to Bruno Walter, the conductor who had been Mahler's disciple and friend for nearly seventeen years.[1] It is a culminating synthesis of song and symphony, two traditionally separate genres that Mahler had begun to intertwine twenty years earlier in his First Symphony, which incorporates material from his *Lieder eines fahrenden Gesellen*. Moreover, *Das Lied* is a fusion of breadth and detail, of overall horizon and splendid immediacy, that he was never to surpass. It is perhaps Mahler's most poignant and intimate utterance upon the religious and philosophical issues that he pursued, and was pursued by, throughout his life and creative work. And as he wrote Bruno Walter in September 1908, when the work was finished but not yet named, "I myself do not know how to express what the whole thing might be called. A beautiful time was granted me, and I believe it is the most personal thing I have yet created."[2]

The problem of the title was probably due in part to the work's interfusion of genres (song and symphony). But the more personal reason for his hesitation, according to several contemporaries, was a superstitious fear of a Ninth Symphony – the last such work for both Beethoven and Bruckner. As Walter puts it, Mahler "did not care to challenge fate."[3] For as is well known, fate had dealt severely with Mahler during 1907: his departure from the Vienna Court Opera, the death of his elder daughter,

---

[1] Bruno Walter, *Gustav Mahler*, trans. James Galston (New York, 1941; repr. 1973), 124.
[2] *Gustav Mahler: Briefe*, rev. and enl. edn. by Herta Blaukopf (Vienna, 1982) [hereinafter *GMB2*], no. 400; also found in *Selected Letters of Gustav Mahler*, ed. Knud Martner, trans. Eithne Wilkins, Ernst Kaiser, and Bill Hopkins (New York, 1979) [hereinafter *GMBE*], no. 378, early September 1908.   [3] Walter, *Mahler*, Eng. trans., 58–59.

the diagnosis of his heart problem, and the move to a new position in the New World were all events that transformed his life at deepest levels. In a letter to Walter during the composition of *Das Lied*, he put it thus: "I stood vis à vis de rien and now at the end of a life I must learn to stand and move again as a beginner."[4]

Asked at the age of four or five what he wanted to be when he grew up, the future composer of the "Resurrection" Symphony replied: "A martyr!"[5] And from earliest childhood he associated concrete ideas with all music: for Beethoven's "Kakadu" piano trio (variations on the tune "I am the tailor Kakadu"), for example, the boy Mahler invented a program of the tailor's entire life, right up to the grave.[6] His own life and work became a lasting symbiotic union – "only when I experience do I 'compose,' and only when I compose do I experience!" he declared in 1897.[7] And it seems clear that he envisioned his symphonies as an oeuvre, a gradually evolving totality. Thus it is scarcely surprising that in 1908 he would create a work both personal and valedictory. In 1895 Mahler had formulated his now-famous definition of the symphony as "to build a world with all the resources of the available techniques," and he reiterated the essence of this view when he met Sibelius in the fall of 1907: "the symphony must be like the world. It must embrace everything."[8] The events of that year made Mahler more aware than ever that his next effort might be his last. To better grasp the nature of the work he eventually called *The Song of the Earth*, and especially how and to what it bids adieu in its extraordinary finale, "Der Abschied," we must survey Mahler's symphonic worlds to that point, despite the shortcomings of necessary brevity: that is the purpose of the first chapter. Following the general plan of the Cambridge Music Handbooks series, succeeding chapters present a history of the music's genesis, an account of its reception, and a reading of the work from both large and local perspectives.

---

[4] *GMB2*, no. 396 (*GMBE*, no. 375), 18 July 1908.

[5] Alma Mahler, preface to the first edn. of Mahler's letters, in *GMB2*, xiv (*GMBE*, 25).

[6] From the manuscripts of Natalie Bauer-Lechner's "Mahleriana," printed in Norman Lebrecht, *Mahler Remembered* (New York, 1988), 14.

[7] *GMB2*, no. 216 (*GMBE*, no. 205), 17 February 1897.

[8] Natalie Bauer-Lechner, *Gustav Mahler in den Erinnerungen von Natalie Bauer-Lechner*, ed. Herbert Killian, with annotations by Knud Martner (Hamburg, 1984) [hereinafter *NBL2*], 35; also found in *Recollections of Gustav Mahler*, trans. Dika Newlin, ed. Peter Franklin (Cambridge, 1980) [hereinafter *NBLE*], 40, summer 1895; Karl Ekman, *Jean Sibelius: His Life and Personality*, trans. Edward Birse (New York, 1938), 190–91.

A few notes on practical matters are in order. (1) The orchestral score of *Das Lied* has been frequently reprinted, but only one edition (the Kritische Gesamtausgabe) contains bar numbers: accordingly, references to specific passages are here made by rehearsal cue in boldface, followed by the number of bars before or after the cue – e. g., fig. **5** + 2 means the second bar after the barline over which figure **5** appears; **5** − 2 indicates two bars before the figure. (2) Translations are mine except when an endnote cites only a source in English. I do, however, acknowledge the aid of previous translations even if I have not agreed with them. (3) The text of *Das Lied von der Erde* has been well translated into English several times; a particularly elegant version is that by Deryck Cooke, which appears (with minor amendments) in Donald Mitchell's detailed discussion of the work.[9] Accordingly, the translation offered in the Appendix is rather different: an interlinear alignment of the German with literal English equivalents. While this gives rise to some strange locutions, I hope it will enable readers with limited knowledge of German to enjoy Mahler's excellent setting of the poetry. (4) A list of the bibliographic abbreviations used in the endnotes appears on page xiv.

Many people have contributed to the emergence of this volume, and I wish to thank them all (with apologies to those not here named). Robert Bailey first introduced me to Mahler scholarship, and many ideas from his seminars as well as his unpublished paper on *Das Lied von der Erde* are reflected in these pages.[10] Edward R. Reilly and R. Larry Todd were instrumental in my taking up the study of Mahler manuscripts, and particularly in the rediscovery of Mahler's voice-and-piano autograph of *Das Lied*. To the owner of that manuscript I am deeply grateful for permission to study and publish it. The growing family of Mahler specialists has been helpful and encouraging, and I especially wish to thank Henry-Louis de La Grange and the staff of the Bibliothèque Gustav Mahler, Paris; the Internationale Gustav Mahler Gesellschaft in Vienna (Herta Blaukopf, Emmy Hauswirth, Morton Solvik, and their colleagues); Donald Mitchell, London; Stuart Feder, New York; Knud Martner,

[9] Deryck Cooke, *Gustav Mahler: An Introduction to His Music* (London, 1980); Donald Mitchell, *Gustav Mahler*, vol. III: *Songs and Symphonies of Life and Death* (Berkeley, 1985) [hereinafter *SSLD*].

[10] Robert Bailey, "*Das Lied von der Erde*: Tonal Language and Formal Design," paper presented to the Forty-Fourth Annual Meeting of the American Musicological Society, Minneapolis, October 1978, and also to the Colorado MahlerFest, Boulder, January 1998.

Copenhagen; Reinhold Brinkmann, Harvard University; Klaus G. Roy, Cleveland, Ohio, who generously offered numerous refinements; Steven Bruns, University of Colorado, Boulder; and Gilbert E. Kaplan, New York. Research contributing to the volume was conducted during several visits to Vienna that were variously supported by a Martha Baird Rockefeller Grant-in-Aid for Musicology, a Morse Fellowship for Junior Faculty at Yale University, a Griswold Grant for research abroad from Yale University, and a Research Grant from the American Philosophical Society. I sincerely thank them all.

This handbook evolved from lectures and seminars given at Stanford, Yale, and Case Western Reserve Universities as well as at the Oberlin College Conservatory, and I am grateful to the many students who responded thoughtfully to them. Some of the material presented here appears in more condensed format in *The Mahler Companion*, edited by Donald Mitchell and Andrew Nicholson (Oxford, 1999); my thanks to them and also to editors at Cambridge University Press for consenting to the inevitable overlap. I am especially grateful to my colleague at Case Western Reserve University, Peter Yang, for making the translation of the poem by Li-Po presented in Chapter 2. With her customary enthusiasm, Maria McLeeson of Cleveland kindly checked the translations and summaries from German reviews of the work's premiere as well as the interlinear translation in the Appendix. Bill Milhoan and Francy Acosta at the CWRU Center for Music and Technology assisted in arranging the text of the translation. And I am particularly indebted to Penny Souster, music editor of Cambridge University Press, and Julian Rushton, general editor of this series, for their kind patience in awaiting the completion of this volume. Lucy Carolan and Michelle Williams at Cambridge were most helpful during its production.

For permission to reproduce the plates presented here I thank the Bibliothèque Gustav Mahler, Paris; the current owner of Mahler's voice-and-piano autograph of *Das Lied*; and the Gemeentemuseum in The Hague. Other libraries helpful in the study of sources pertaining to *Das Lied* are: The Pierpont Morgan Library, New York (J. Rigbie Turner, curator of music manuscripts); the archive of the Gesellschaft der Musikfreunde, Vienna (Otto Biba, director); the Österreichische Nationalbibliothek (especially Christa Traunsteiner); and the Stadt- und Landesbibliothek, Vienna. And I am grateful, as always, to the Kulas

Music Library at CWRU (Stephen H. Toombs, librarian) and the library of the Cleveland Institute of Music (Jean Toombs, librarian). I thank as well *The Journal of Musicology* (Marian Green, editor) for permission to reproduce diagrams and a table from my article on the piano version of the work.

Abbreviations

GMB2   *Gustav Mahler: Briefe.* Revised and enlarged edition by
Herta Blaukopf. Vienna, 1982.

GMBE   *Selected Letters of Gustav Mahler.* Edited by Knud Martner.
Translated by Eithne Wilkins, Ernst Kaiser, and Bill
Hopkins. New York, 1979.

HLG 1   De La Grange, Henry-Louis. *Mahler.* Vol. I. Garden City,
1973.

HLG 2   *Gustav Mahler.* Vol. II: *Vienna: The Years of Challenge
(1897–1904).* Oxford, 1995.

HLGF   De La Grange, Henry-Louis. *Gustav Mahler: Chronique
d'une vie.* 3 vols. Paris, 1979–84.

NBL2   Bauer-Lechner, Natalie. *Gustav Mahler in den Erinnerungen
von Natalie Bauer-Lechner.* Edited by Herbert Killian,
with annotations by Knud Martner. Hamburg, 1984.

NBLE   *Recollections of Gustav Mahler.* Translated by Dika
Newlin. Edited by Peter Franklin. Cambridge, 1980.

SSLD   Mitchell, Donald. *Gustav Mahler.* Vol. III: *Songs and
Symphonies of Life and Death.* Berkeley and Los
Angeles, 1985.

Background: Mahler's "symphonic worlds" before 1908

Tragedy and the hope of redemption: Schopenhauer, Wagner, Nietzsche, Lipiner

Fundamental to an understanding of Mahler's work as a whole is the Schopenhauerian worldview, embraced and extended by Wagner and Nietzsche, in which Mahler was steeped from his student days in Vienna (1875–83). And a crucial figure in his intellectual development during the ensuing quarter-century was the brilliant young poet-philosopher Siegfried Lipiner (1856–1911), whose early writings are directly derived from the ideas of the three authors just named. Even in later years Mahler continued to cite Schopenhauer's *The World as Will and Representation* (1819/1844) and Wagner's "Beethoven" essay (1870, commemorating the composer's centenary) as the most profound writings on music he knew.[1] To these we need to add a third volume based on those two, Nietzsche's *The Birth of Tragedy from the Spirit of Music* (1872), plus a related lecture by Lipiner cited below.

Briefly summarized, the overall viewpoint these writers espouse is as follows: The world, which is experienced as representation, is, in itself, *will* – "the innermost essence, the kernel of every particular thing, and also of the whole."[2] Schopenhauerian will is the blind force of nature, yet also the driving force of human beings (akin in many respects to Freud's notion of the id). Humanity is deceived by the *principium individuationis*, the principle of individuation which is the form of phenomena; as a result, we live out an endlessly egoistic cycle in which desires of the will can be at best only partially fulfilled. Dissatisfaction ensues, and the cycle recurs – it is the punishing, perpetually rolling wheel of Ixion (to which Mahler referred in comments about the Third Symphony).[3] "Birth and death belong equally to life, and hold the balance as mutual conditions of each other – poles of the whole phenomenon of life." That is the reason, Schopenhauer says, that Indian mythology gives the god Shiva, who represents destruction and death, both a necklace of skulls and the *lingam*, or phallus – the symbol of procreation that appears as the counterpart of death.[4] For Schopenhauer there were only two sources of relief from the wheel of Ixion: the effect of grace occurring in Christian or Buddhist religion, and the temporary stilling of the will that results from dispassionate aesthetic contemplation of the arts.[5] But music, he asserts, is the highest of the arts because it is the direct and immediate expression of the will, without intervening conceptualizations; it "never expresses the phenomenon, but only the inner nature . . . We could just as well call the world embodied music as embodied will."[6] On such a view, of course, true music could not be program music in the ordinary sense that we think of it, because stories are conceptualizations of phenomena.

In *The Birth of Tragedy from the Spirit of Music,* Nietzsche transposes the duality of will and representation into passionate Dionysian abandon versus harmonious Apollonian restraint. Dionysian art gives expression to the will in its omnipotence – the eternal life beyond all phenomena, and despite all annihilation: this was the Dionysian wisdom of Greek tragedy, which Nietzsche claims to be born from the spirit of music, which is the immediate manifestation of the will. The tragic, titanic hero is "negated for our pleasure," as Nietzsche puts it, "because he is only phenomenon, and because the eternal life of the will is not affected by his annihilation . . . music is the immediate idea of this life."[7] Music gives birth to tragic myth, and "tragedy absorbs the highest ecstasies of music, so that it truly brings music . . . to its perfection."[8] For Nietzsche, "all that comes into being must be ready for a sorrowful end; we are forced to look into the terrors of the individual existence – yet we are not to become rigid with fear . . ." The "maddening sting of these pains" pierces us just at the moment when, in Dionysian ecstasy, we anticipate the indestructibility and eternity of infinite primordial joy.[9]

Siegfried Lipiner had fully absorbed and expounded upon the Nietzschean concept of tragedy during Mahler's years at the Vienna Conservatory. In his lecture "On the Elements of a Renewal of Religious Ideas in the Present" published in 1878, Lipiner declares that in tragedy, we suffer to the extreme, then, only bleeding, man wrests himself from his transitory self, and in [tragedy] the joy of all joys rushes through us, for in this bleeding tearing-oneself-away we feel the omnipotence and magnificence of the higher self, our own godliness . . . here the truest son of Prometheus, proud and daring, as never before, may praise the divinity, for he himself is become this divinity. Here and only here are death and time overcome, here and only here are the sting of pain and victory of hell torn away . . . The giant Pain is here – and only here – properly finished; it overcomes the giant I.[10]

Not at all coincidentally, these last lines are closely linked to verses Mahler himself penned for the gigantic chorus-and-soloists finale of his Second Symphony:

> O believe, my heart, O believe:
> Yours is . . . what you longed for!
> Yours, what you loved,
> what you struggled for:
> . . . .
> O Pain! You all-penetrating one!
> From you I have broken away!
> O Death! You all-conquering one!
> Now you are conquered!
> With wings which I have won for myself
> in fervent striving of Love
> I will soar . . .
> . . . .
> I will die in order to live!

Moreover, in an essay published just before Mahler wrote his first two symphonies, Lipiner also presents a view of the relation between creativity and personality that, on all available evidence, is congruent with Mahler's own:

For he himself [i. e., the poet] is only an example of his kind; and just as he will never set forth as poetry an isolated or chance event, the amorphous rock of so-called reality merely as he found it, so will his own personal experience become for him at best an opportune cause to create a type, which will explain to thousands what *they* are feeling. Verily, he will never see by means of the flickering fire of personal passion, but rather with the light of a quiet, warm sun that ranges over everything and everyone; and then he will create what he has seen, in that form which appears to him best to convey what is unexpressed of "life": with the ruling spirit, even if with ever so striving heart, – always conquered by truth, never tyrannized by reality.[11]

Programmatic metaphors: the tetralogy of the first four symphonies

In August 1900 Mahler finished the drafts of his Fourth Symphony, which concludes with a poem from *Des Knaben Wunderhorn* – "Das himmlische Leben" ("Heavenly Life"), as Mahler had re-titled it – to be sung by a solo soprano "with bright childlike expression, entirely without parody," according to the score. A greater contrast to the escha- tological epic of the Second Symphony's finale would be difficult to imagine. Yet Mahler seriously claimed to his longtime confidante and chronicler, Natalie Bauer-Lechner, that "as regards content and form" his first four symphonies are "a thoroughly self-contained tetralogy."[12] How this could be so emerges only from close reading of both the music and Mahler's various metaphorical remarks about it, which frequently constitute programmatic outlines of the sort he once characterized as "a few milestones and signposts for the journey – or, shall we say, a star map in order to comprehend the night sky with all its luminous worlds."[13] These commentaries indeed reveal that Mahler based his music in no small part on the type of artistic vision and distillation of personal expe- rience advocated by Lipiner. To be sure, in October 1900 Mahler would make a now-famous toast known as the "Munich Declaration" con- demning descriptive programs, and thereafter he usually (although not invariably) forbade public distribution of programmatic commentary about his music.[14] But as noted above, since childhood he had associated music with concrete ideas, and privately, among people he trusted, such as Natalie Bauer-Lechner and Bruno Walter, Mahler continued to speak about his music in metaphors that, if not overtaxed, can provide useful insight into the works that form the background for *Das Lied von der Erde*.[15]

4

Werther becomes Prometheus: the First Symphony and "Todtenfeier"

Indeed, it was Bruno Walter who characterized the First Symphony as "Mahler's *Werther*."[16] The Werther theme of unrequited love and suicide had already been the subject of Mahler's *Lieder eines fahrenden Gesellen* (*Songs of a Wayfarer*), based on poetry he had written in the wake of an unhappy affair with the soprano Johanna Richter in 1884–85. In the case of the First, the object of his illicit affection was Marion von Weber (wife of the grandson of Carl Maria von Weber, the famous composer), and Mahler's substantial borrowings from song cycle to symphony underscore both the nature and the intensity of his feeling. Such a triadic interaction of love, depression, and artistic response would repeatedly spur Mahler's output from the time of *Das klagende Lied* (1880) through the unfinished Tenth Symphony (1910).[17]

Mahler's commentaries on the First Symphony assume the perspective of "the hero," his artistically projected persona (Lipiner's "example of his kind") engaged in a drama of Promethean conflict. The hero's moods and experiences progress from the shimmering awakening of nature and "Dionysian jubilation" of the first movement, through the lamenting and bitterly ironic funereal vision based on "Frère Jacques" in the minor mode, to searing heartbreak and fearful struggle with all the sorrow of the world in the finale – "Dall'Inferno" ("Out of Hell") as he at one point entitled it. Later Mahler described the symphony's finale to Natalie, who recorded the discussion as follows:

> "Again and again he [the hero] receives a blow to the head from fate – and with him the victory motive," just when he seems to have raised himself above fate and become its master, and only in death – since he has conquered himself, and the wonderful concord of his youth suddenly reemerges with the theme of the first movement – does he achieve the victory. (Magnificent victory chorale!)[18]

Yet characteristically for Mahler, before the First was complete, he was seized in January 1888 by the inspiration for its polar opposite, the tragic "Todtenfeier" movement ("Funeral Rites," or literally "Celebration of the Dead") that would eventually open the Second Symphony. Stricken by one of the visions that occasionally overcame him while composing, "He saw himself lying dead on a bier under wreaths and flowers (which were in his room from the performance of the *Pintos*), until Frau von Weber quickly took all flowers away from him."[19] At one level, such anxiety is scarcely surprising: the flowers were in celebration of Mahler's first major success as a composer-conductor, his completion of Carl Maria von Weber's unfinished opera *Die drei Pintos* – made from sketches inherited by Marion's husband and entrusted by him to Mahler. But Mahler's terrified vision was also intertwined with the harrowing figure of a Werther *sub specie aeternitatis* (under the semblance of eternity), also named Gustav, who appears in Adam Mickiewicz's dramatic epic *Dziady*, which Siegfried Lipiner had published in German translation – entitled *Todtenfeier* – the previous year.[20] In his lengthy introduction, Lipiner asserts that Gustav's suicide represents nothing less than "*the Fall of Man* and its punishment"[21] – and in his (and Mahler's) view, such Promethean defiance must lead towards transcendence. At the shattering dissonant climax of the "Todtenfeier" movement, Mahler draws again upon musical rhetoric from his *Lieder eines fahrenden Gesellen*, this time expanding upon gestures of the explicitly suicidal third song, "Ich hab' ein glühend Messer" ("I Have a Burning Knife"). But it would take him another six years to hit upon the fitting conclusion to this defiant dramatic opening – a finale based, as we have seen, on the notion of redemption through tragic suffering. Nevertheless, Mahler's characteristic creative pattern of dialectic interaction between syzygial opposites in the search for higher meaning was now well established; as Bruno Walter so rightly observes,

> For him there was fundamentally never release from the sorrowful struggle over the meaning of human existence . . . "For what" remained the agonizing question of his soul. From this arose the strongest spiritual impulses for his creativity, each of his works was a new attempt at an answer. And when he had won the answer for himself, the old question soon raised its unassuageable call of longing in him anew. He could not – such was his nature – hold fast to any achieved spiritual position, for he himself was not constant.[22]

Nowhere is this more evident than in the contrast between the monumentally triumphant "Symphony of a Thousand" and the work that follows it, *Das Lied von der Erde*.

The "Budapest stagnation"

Mahler composed very little between September 1888 and January 1892, the period he dubbed his "Budapest stagnation." Yet his world changed in many ways. His driving professional ambition won the twenty-eight-year-old conductor both the prestige and the heavy responsibility of directing the Royal Hungarian Opera in Budapest. He proudly shared news of his accomplishments there with the family back in his provincial hometown of Iglau, but even then the health of his parents was declining rapidly. Their marriage, based on convenience rather than love, had been difficult, and was marked by the deaths of eight children in infancy or childhood. In Mahler's words, his mother and father "got along like fire and ice. He was all stubbornness, she gentleness itself."[23] Parental quarrels and dying siblings had overshadowed his childhood, the time in which, as he several times acknowledged, the raw materials for composing were stored up.[24] Father Bernhard Mahler, who indeed "domineered over his delicate wife and flogged the children" as Alma Mahler puts it,[25] died in February 1889. However ambivalent his feelings toward his father, Mahler's residual conflict in the wake of his death must have been distressing. But his strong emotional attachment to his mother, who followed her husband to the grave in October 1889, is clearly apparent from many sources. As the psychoanalyst Stuart Feder observes, Mahler was doubly loved by Marie Mahler, both as her first surviving child and as the replacement for her firstborn son who had died the year prior to Gustav's birth; it seems clear that Gustav's position of priority among his siblings gave him, in the words of Freud's adage, "the feeling of a conqueror, that confidence of success that often induces real success." Feder continues:

> Mahler's music is repeatedly informed by this primary and enduring relationship in mental life, from his musical identification with the grieving parent of the *Kindertotenlieder* (e. g., the third song, "Wenn dein Mütterlein . . . [When your dear mother . . .]") to the ultimate idealization of the eternal feminine in the Eighth Symphony. Through the transformations of her son's art, modest Marie Hermann was destined to endow representations of the quotidian-tragic mother as well as the most noble symbol of motherhood: Marie become Mary, the Mater Gloriosa of *Faust*.[26]

7

Yet apparently Mahler missed her funeral, remaining in Budapest to rehearse, of all things, *The Merry Wives of Windsor*.[27] The irony is thoroughly Mahlerian.

According to family lore, it was Mahler's mother who had first encouraged him to compose at age six, rewarding him with two *Kreuzer* for a polka with a funeral march as an introduction [!] written not long after the deaths of two younger siblings.[28] How different was the reception of his First Symphony, also graced with an unusual funeral march, in Budapest just five weeks after Marie Mahler died: both critics and audience were outraged, and Mahler "went about as though diseased, or an outlaw."[29] The most objectionable portions were precisely the funeral march and the storm that breaks out after it – the "devilish" music that is most original and characteristically Mahlerian, like portions of the "Todtenfeier" movement. And the condemnation of "Todtenfeier" by Hans von Bülow in 1891 was another painful blow; the famous conductor declared that by comparison to it, *Tristan* was a Haydn symphony.[30]

"Heavenly Life" and "Joyous Science": Mahler blossoms

The "Budapest stagnation" was indeed a low ebb; we know of at least two factors that brought Mahler out of it. One was the "epoch-making influence" of renewed engagement with the writings of Nietzsche late in 1891;[31] the other was reacquaintance with the world of *Des Knaben Wunderhorn* (*From the Boy's Magic Horn*), the Romantic collection of German folk poetry praised as a genuine manifestation of untutored wisdom by writers as diverse as Goethe and Nietzsche. Within just over a year Mahler's *Wunderhorn* "Humoresken," as he called them, would begin to infiltrate the high culture of the symphony through the extraordinary transformation of "Des Antonius von Padua Fischpredigt" ("St. Anthony's Sermon to the Fishes") into the scherzo of the Second Symphony. But the most influential of the *Humoresken* was the first piece that broke his long creative hiatus: "Das himmlische Leben," whose text and deep-reaching music continued to enchant Mahler during the next eight years, until at length he found its proper setting as the finale of his Fourth Symphony. "What roguishness intertwined with the deepest mysticism is hidden in it!" he told Natalie Bauer-Lechner. "It is everything turned on its head, and causality has absolutely no validity. It is as though you

8

suddenly saw the far side of the moon!"[32] While Mahler undoubtedly assumed the text was folk poetry, we now know it to be the work of a single learned writer who laced it with numerous scriptural allusions in paradoxical contexts. The upshot is an instance of *ingénu* irony, whereby the naively innocent protagonist of the poem – a child, in Mahler's setting – utters things whose full import he does not understand. One illustrative instance must here stand for many: in the second strophe of the lied we are told that John the Baptist (i. e., the forerunner of the Lamb of God) turns the Lamb over to Herod (the tetrarch of Galilee who had ordered John beheaded at the behest of Salome): how curious to encounter such violence in a song wherein the second line is: "Kein weltlich' Getümmel hört man nicht in Himmel [One don't hear no worldly tumult in heaven]"![33] This was indeed a new creative avenue for Mahler; to place it in the perspective of his "epoch-making" reading, the lied is a curious sort of "fröhliche Wissenschaft" ("joyous knowledge" or "gay science"), a light, bewinged manifestation of the child, who, for Nietzsche, came to represent "innocence and forgetting, a new beginning, a game, a self-propelled wheel, a first movement, a sacred Yes."[34] In 1901, when the Fourth was finished, Mahler would provide a more traditional interpretation of the singer of "Heavenly Life": "the child, who, although in a chrysalis state [*im Puppenstand*], already belongs to this higher world, clarifies what it all means."[35] To arrive in heaven *im Puppenstand* was the final fate of Goethe's ever-striving Faust, and Mahler associated the same rubric with the singer of "Urlicht" ("Primal Light"), the *Wunderhorn* song he would shortly adopt as a miniature prelude to the vast Resurrection finale that would conclude the Second Symphony. Although he dared not set the famous conclusion of *Faust* until 1906 (in the finale of his Eighth), it would seem that Mahler anticipated a similar fate for his "symphonic hero" as early as 1892. "Das himmlische Leben," then, provided an answer to the despair and stagnation surrounding "Todtenfeier"; the song could not possibly balance that massive C minor first movement as the finale of the Second, but it did act as a beacon, "the tapering spire of the structure," during the composition of his Third and Fourth Symphonies, which comprise the second half of the "self-contained tetralogy."

It is difficult to pinpoint Mahler's further responses to Nietzsche, both because they were mixed, and because that writer's spiraling mode of thought resists facile conceptualization. Quite possibly Nietzsche's stance on traditional religion – that God is dead, and therefore humanity is to anticipate the *Übermensch* – gave Mahler the courage to conclude the Second Symphony with his unorthodox vision of resurrection, which takes place through the rather Romantic agency of "wings which I have won for myself in fervent striving of Love," according to Mahler's own poetry, rather than through divine grace. But Mahler's universalism – "no divine judgment, no blessed and no damned; no good, no evil ones, no judge!" – is almost certainly derived from Lipiner's teacher, Gustav Theodor Fechner, who taught that

> there is no heaven and no hell in the usual sense of the Christian, the Jew, the heathen, into which the soul may enter . . . after it has passed through the great transition, death, it unfolds itself according to the unalterable law of nature upon earth . . . quietly approaching and entering into a higher existence.[36]

As we shall see, Fechner's views were also influential in Mahler's shaping of *Das Lied von der Erde*.

The famous "lightning bolt" of inspiration for the Second's finale that struck Mahler in March 1894 at the memorial service – publicly announced as a "Todten-Feier" – for Hans von Bülow, who had severely condemned Mahler's "Todtenfeier" movement, is among the best-known events in his career. The psychoanalyst Theodor Reik has insisted upon the Oedipal aspect of this extraordinary breakthrough in Mahler's creative logjam; Reik's view, if overstated, contains a kernel of truth.[37] Between 1888 and 1894 Mahler wrestled inwardly or overtly with several oppressive patriarchal authority figures: the Judeo-Christian God, his earthly father Bernhard, his supervisor Bernhard Pollini, director of the Hamburg Opera (the "Pollini jail" as Mahler called it), Hans von Bülow – and not least, Beethoven, whose apotheosis of joy in the Ninth Symphony Mahler both imitated and challenged in his "Resurrection" finale. Nevertheless, it was the success of the Second among audiences (if not, initially, among critics) that first made Mahler a significant European composer of the day.

In the First and Second Symphonies Mahler establishes several broad characteristics of his symphonic oeuvre as a whole. First is the principle of the "frame" (as Donald Mitchell has lately dubbed it), derived from

Beethoven, whereby the first and last movements respectively introduce and resolve (at least temporarily) the main issues of the symphony, and the two or more inner movements are rather like interludes. In the First Mahler had originally grouped the five movements into larger blocks that he labeled "Abtheilung[en]"; a similar arrangement is explicitly indicated in the Third and Fifth Symphonies, and is fundamental to *Das Lied von der Erde* (although not marked as such in the score). As Mahler once told Natalie, "Composing is like playing with bricks, whereby a new building always arises from the same stones. The stones, however, have lain there ready and waiting from one's youth, the only time for collecting and storing them."[38] And a prime musical topos found in virtually all his symphonies is the march, a predilection doubtless stemming from his childhood experiences in the barracks town of Iglau.[39] Marches are humanity on the move – into the heat of combat, home in the glory of victory (or shame of defeat), or solemnly en route to the final resting place; Mahler draws upon all varieties. Another common movement type is the folksy Austrian Ländler, which Mahler came to know from Schubert and Bruckner as well as from popular music. And as noted, he also incorporates into the large, public genre of the symphony that most intimate and private of Romantic musical forms, the lied, drawing upon folk poetry as well. Also from Mahler's childhood grows his Romantic fascination with the sounds, moods, and atmospheres associated with nature that he molds into music, sometimes specifically calling them *Naturlaute*. Indeed, from the summer of 1893, when he resumed work on the Second, through the end of his career, an isolated summer *Häuschen* (composing hut) in the country, or better yet in the woods, was essential for the inspiration to compose.

His sense of affective association with specific tonalities is both traditional and idiosyncratic: D major for the "magnificent victory" of the First and C minor as the tragic key of "Todtenfeier" are stock in trade, whereas E major is a pastoral, blissful key, as in the contrasting second subject of "Todtenfeier" and the serene close of "Das himmlische Leben." He deploys the full resources of advanced nineteenth-century tonal practice, including third-relations, "expressive" tonality (whole- or semitone ascents to suggest brightness and intensification, the opposite for depression or darkening affect),[40] irregular cadential resolutions, chromaticism and surface dissonance, etc. Yet the overall framework of tonality remains solidly apparent, based on traditional voice-leading techniques. In the early symphonies Mahler's developmental procedures tend to favor drama and gesture more than compact motivic working-out; beginning with the Fourth he would achieve a more impressive balance. And Mahler's sensitive and imaginative treatment of the orchestra, from which he draws sharply characterized colors, is already fully apparent in these two works.

Finally, we should take note of an archetypal musical motive in the finale of the Second that would recur in many of Mahler's subsequent works, including *Das Lied*: the "Ewigkeit" ("eternity") motive (Ex. 1). Borrowed from Wagner's *Siegfried*, where it is associated with the word "Ewig" ("eternal[ly]"), it is deployed by Mahler in a variety of contexts, but always with connotations of temporal transcendence, and frequently suggesting ascent to a realm of peace and nurturance, such as the sphere of "das Ewig-Weibliche" ("the eternal feminine") in the Eighth Symphony, and in numerous other works.[41]

A second syzygial pair: the Third and Fourth Symphonies

"Meine fröhliche Wissenschaft" ("My Joyous Science"): the Third Symphony

Mahler's next two symphonies share a common origin: "Das himmlische Leben," which he at first planned to serve as finale of the Third. Only when he realized the vast proportions to which that wide-ranging symphonic world had sprawled did he transfer the child's vision of paradise to an entirely different work, conceived in concise neoclassical style. Mahler's Third is a vast pantheistic meditation on the evolution of the world from primeval nature through man to the realm of divinity. Its six movements last ninety minutes or more, and the music is replete with sonic symbols of nature – "Pan asleep," "The southern gale," "The bird of the night," etc. – specifically labeled in the autograph score. Particularly in the huge first movement, a "Pan-inspired abundance" of irrepressibly billowing Dionysian life force, "Mahler takes greater risks than he ever did again," as Adorno observes: "The literary idea of the great god Pan has invaded the sense of form; form itself becomes something both fearful and monstrous, the objectification of chaos . . ."[42]

Example 1   The "Ewigkeit" ("Eternity") motive (a) Wagner, *Siegfried*, act
III, scene 3 (Brünnhilde) (b) Mahler, Second Symphony, finale (c) Mahler,
Second Symphony, finale; text: "I shall die in order to live!"

Both background and genesis of the Third have been well surveyed by
Peter Franklin in a companion volume of the Cambridge Music Handbooks series.[43] For present purposes we should note three points: (1)
Mahler's vision of evolution in the Third Symphony embodies not only
the Schopenhauerian notion of will as blind force of nature, but also
Fechner's view of the cosmos as an inwardly alive spiritual hierarchy
extending from atoms up to God, who "is at once the base and the
summit."[44] Both viewpoints inform *Das Lied* as well. (2) As suggested by
its provisional title, "Meine fröhliche Wissenschaft," the Third also
manifests Mahler's ongoing engagement with Nietzsche, but more especially with his scriptural parody *Thus Spoke Zarathustra*, the book of the
prophet who announces that "God is dead" and, in his famous midnight
song, guardedly reveals and elaborates Nietzsche's doctrine of eternal
recurrence – that everyone must "come back eternally to this same, self-
same life, in what is greatest as in what is smallest."[45] It is precisely
Zarathustra's midnight song that Mahler sets for alto solo as the fourth
movement of the new symphony, "O Man, Take Heed." Then follow
children's and women's voices chiming *Wunderhorn* lyrics on Christian
themes, "Three Angels Were Singing." His explanation of this bold

juxtaposition: "here humor has got to aim for the heights that can no longer be expressed otherwise."[46] But the work concludes with a hymn-like orchestral adagio originally entitled "What Love Tells Me" – the "liberating resolution" in which the Schopenhauerian wheel of Ixion is stilled, according to Mahler.[47] "I could almost also call the movement 'What God tells me!'" he wrote to Anna von Mildenburg (the soprano who was then his lover). "And this in precisely the sense that God can only be comprehended as 'Love.'"[48] According to Alfred Roller (Mahler's revolutionary set designer at the Vienna Opera, 1903–07), "His faith was that of a child. God is love and love is God. This idea came up a thousand times in his conversation."[49] It is not, however, a common notion in late Nietzsche. Finally (3), Mahler's personal identification with this symphony was yet more intense than with the previous two, and often terrifying, as though he were confronted by

> the Universe itself, into whose immeasurable void you plunge, in whose eternal space you whirl, such that earth and human fate fall behind you like a tiny speck and vanish. The highest questions of humanity, which I posed in the Second and tried to answer: Why do we live, and will we survive beyond this life? – here these can no longer concern me. For what can that mean in a Universe where everything *lives* and *must* and *will* live?[50]

In certain passages he feared the work "has almost ceased to be music; it is almost just sounds of nature."[51] And Mahler was equally aware of its numerous appropriations of plebeian music: "Often one would believe he were in a lowly pub or a stable," he wrote Bruno Walter.[52] The boy of four who professed he wanted to become a martyr was now the mature master confident in his powers yet fearful of both "the path that music must follow" in his hands, and the abuse he would consequently suffer. Mahler compared his martyrdom to

> Christ on the Mount of Olives, who had to drain the chalice of sorrow to the dregs – and willed it so. He for whom this chalice is destined can and will not refuse it, but death-agony must at times overcome him when he thinks of what still lies before him.[53]

Yet such a messianic self-identification represents more than humble servitude. It is closely allied both to his "intense narcissistic interest in his post-life," as Feder puts it,[54] and to a Nietzschean usurpation of tradition and authority that is also distinctly Oedipal. As he copied out the full score of the Third's first movement in 1896, Mahler likened the piece to "Zeus destroying Kronos" as well as to Jacob wrestling with God for divine blessing: "God also wants not to bless me; only in fearful struggle over the coming into being of my works do I wrest it from him."[55]

During the following year Mahler also managed to wrest control of the Vienna Court Opera from its first conductor, Hans Richter, and its aging director, Wilhelm Jahn, again astonishing the musical world by his meteoric success at a relatively young age (thirty-seven). Vienna had always been his goal, and he was determined to show what he could do. He had long since become a tyrant in the pit of the theatre; during his last year in Hamburg he admitted to Bauer-Lechner that

> I can only make it work in the role of an animal trainer, which I assume there, one who constantly lays on the lash of the most taxing demands upon their attentiveness and capacity for work, and who handles them the roughest when the beast of impotence and indolence ventures forth even for a moment.[56]

He drove himself just as relentlessly, sometimes to the point of ill-health; hemorrhoids, migraines, and sore throats were common ailments, and what little free time he had during the summer of 1897 was devoted to convalescence.

Moodiness was by now a fixed feature of his personality; during the previous year Natalie had recorded that

> I had never seen in anyone else such change of mood in the most dizzying sequence. His relationship with the people closest to him was also subject to this changeability, which jumped from the most passionate "for" to the most vehement "against," and which could overwhelm a person just as one-sidedly with his love as it could unjustly with his hatred . . .
>
> Recently he came to pick me up at a friend's, and rushed into the house like a whirlwind; he was talkative and in a most sparkling mood, and in his boisterousness and scintillating merriness swept everything along with him. But within a very short time – who knows what went through his head – he suddenly became as silent as the grave, sat there immersed in himself, and said not another word until we left.
>
> His changeability and inconstancy was so great that he never remained

the same for an hour at a time, and everything around and beyond him, but particularly those closest to him, always appeared different in his altered outlook.[57]

Even his physical appearance could change dramatically within days or hours, from youthfulness to the look of a man much older than he was. Today some psychologists suspect he suffered from cyclothymic disorder, a chronic, fluctuating mood disturbance involving numerous periods of hypomanic and depressive symptoms (which symptoms are, however, less numerous or severe than those of the bipolar disorders).[58] In any case, Mahler himself recognized that his creativity was "closely linked with irritability [*Irritabilität*]," and such rapid shifts of mood, from "flowery Elysian fields" to "the nocturnal terrors of Tartarus," are also characteristic of his compositions.[59]

"What the Child Tells Me": the Fourth Symphony

The Fourth is just such a radical shift, from the cosmic monumentality of his previous two works to a quasi-classical four-movement symphony of about half their length, scored for more modest forces. An Apollonian rather than a Dionysian work, the Fourth was literally "composed into" its preexistent finale, "Das himmlische Leben." And the title that song previously bore as part of the Third – "What the Child Tells Me" – might well be extended to the entire Fourth, for the gently ironic perspective of the *ingénu* infuses the whole. Formally, it is a delicate sendup of symphonic grandeur as in the tradition of Beethoven's Ninth (and Mahler's "Resurrection"): not a profound chorus, but rather a simple child singing a *Wunderhorn* text concludes the proceedings. The point is also underscored by the preceding slow movement, a double variation set culminating in fanfare summonses to a higher realm, just as in the Adagio of Beethoven's Ninth. And as in that icon, Mahler's scherzo with double trio is somewhat terrifying: its tuned-up solo violin is intended to "sound raw and screeching, 'as though Death were striking up'" – an allusion to the ancient German folk figure Freund Hain, the grim reaper, occasionally represented with a fiddle.[60]

As Adorno has emphasized, "The entire Fourth Symphony shuffles nonexistent children's songs together . . . The means are reduced, without heavy brass . . . No father figures are admitted to its precincts."[61]

Such an impression is owing in large measure to Mahler's almost cyclical dispersal of "Himmlisches Leben" motives throughout the work. Overall, Adorno argues, "the symphony is a solitary attempt at musical communication with the déjà vu, in genuine color . . . a spacious fantasy realm in which everything seems to happen once again."[62] And further: "everything is composed within quotation marks . . ."[63] Such capacity to make music conjure forth the past is among the most important features Mahler develops further in his late style, especially in *Das Lied*.

But the Fourth's childlike dimensions are by no means musically regressive. *Au contraire*, like the text of the finale, the music's outward simplicity barely masks its extraordinary sophistication: as never before, Mahler is here the master of development and counterpoint, an advance in technique that would prove essential in the works to come. And in the slow movement, which both he and Richard Strauss regarded as the high point of the Fourth, Mahler achieves a new expressive intimacy by appropriating childhood memories of maternal love, death, and peaceful isolation. As Natalie reports his private commentary,

> "A divinely serene and deeply sad melody runs throughout, at which you will both smile and weep."
>
> He also said that it bore the countenance of St. Ursula (who is sung about in the "Heavenly Life" of the fourth movement). . . .
>
> At one point he also called the Andante the smile of St. Ursula, and said that in it there had hovered before him the face of his mother from childhood, with deep sadness, and as though smiling through tears; she suffered unendingly, yet always lovingly resolved and forgave everything.[64]

Mahler also likened the smile of the mother-saint to the expression of figures found on monuments in ancient churches: "they have the scarcely noticeable, peaceful smile of the slumbering, departed children of mankind . . ."[65] Just such a moment is the movement's close (fig. 13 ff.), which leads directly to the child's celestial song. This passage is marked "sehr zart und innig [very sweetly and intimately]," and notably, at the very end, "gänzlich ersterbend [dying away entirely]": the "Ewigkeit" motive is prominent (cf. Ex. 1), as is a gesture of quiet collapse (fig. 13 + 13 ff.). Variants upon this extraordinary passage soon found their way into two deeply contemplative pieces written the following year (1901): the Rückert lied "Ich bin der Welt abhanden gekommen [I have become lost

17

to the world]" and the famous Adagietto of the Fifth Symphony, composed as a declaration of love for his future wife Alma (see below). Both
are important predecessors of "Der Abschied," the finale of *Das Lied*.

As a child, Mahler would frequently remain motionless in one spot for
hours on end, "lost to the world" in daydreaming, music, and later, literature. Both Natalie and Alma relate the story of young Gustav's taking a
walk in the woods with his father; having forgotten something at home,
Bernhard told the boy to sit on a log until he returned. Back home, as
usual, was "noise, commotion, distraction," and Gustav was completely
forgotten until twilight. The child, meanwhile, had remained sitting
motionless just as his father had left him, "his eyes peacefully lost in
thought, without fear or astonishment. And several hours had passed
before evening fell."[66] While such dreaminess was one way of dodging
childhood traumas, it also generated conflict – in reality, and probably in
fantasy as well. Mahler told Natalie that although he was tormented for
his brooding and felt guilty about it, he later realized it had been essential
to his spiritual development.[67] Psychoanalysts have suggested that such
concentrated stillness as a way of avoiding conflict and fear of abandonment may provoke fantasies anticipating the stillness of death, and of
return to the womb as the ultimate punishment; the flipside, however, is
the craving to overcome fears of abandonment and death through withdrawal and womb-like isolation that approaches claustrophilia, such as
Mahler found in his summer *Häuschen*.[68] In his entire oeuvre, the most
extended and extraordinary passage of music "lost to the world" is of
course the close of *Das Lied von der Erde*, also marked "gänzlich ersterbend" at the end. Alma Mahler, who learned this music from her
husband at the keyboard, suggests that

> with wondrous consequence his inner life returns to the visionary child-
> hood scene in the woods. Is not his farewell [*Abschied*], the "Song of the
> Earth," the ripe fruit of that far-off melancholy contemplation, whose
> kernel may have come to life in the waiting boy?[69]

1901: a year of transitions fundamental to *Das Lied von der Erde*

Except for 1907, the first year of the new century brought more fundamental changes to Mahler's life than any other. From Christmas 1900

through the following February he drove himself ever more relentlessly, despite recurrent headaches, stomachaches, tonsilitis, and hemorrhoid problems. On 24 February he collapsed from a severe hemorrhoidal hemorrhage, having conducted the Vienna Philharmonic at midday and the Opera in the evening. The composer who had so often wrestled with the mysteries of death and eternity believed that "my last hour had come."[70] But Mahler survived. While recovering on holiday, he recounted to Natalie two vivid and terrifying dreams he had remembered for years as the two of them walked in the moonlight beside a mountain lake. The first had occurred when he was only eight years old: the stars engulfed each other in a sky filled with yellow smoke as though it were the end of the world, and the uncanny figure of the Wandering Jew tried to force Mahler to take his staff (topped with a golden cross), the symbol of his eternal wandering; the boy woke with a scream. The second, from 1891, went as follows:

> He found himself in the midst of a large gathering in a brightly lit room, when the last of the guests entered – a large man of stiff bearing, faultlessly dressed, and with the air of a man of affairs. But he [Mahler] knew: that is Death . . . The stranger seized him by the arm with an iron grip and said, "You must come with me! [*Du mußt mit mir!*]" . . .he could not tear himself loose until, by expending all his forces, he threw the nightmare off.[71]

In wake of this illness Mahler's life and work were completely transformed. Within less than a year the bachelor of long standing had become engaged to Alma Schindler, nearly twenty years his junior, and the couple conceived a child prior to their marriage. This rush into the renewal of life was almost certainly in response to his brush with death, as Feder observes. But months before his crucial encounter with Alma, Mahler memorialized that moment artistically during the summer of 1901, in several musical meditations upon death: the last of the *Wunderhorn* songs, three of the *Kindertotenlieder* (*Songs on the Death of Children*), two of the separate Rückert songs, and the beginnings of the Fifth Symphony.[72]

Never again would Mahler draw near the naively humorous world of "Das himmlische Leben." All of his Rückert settings assume an individuated first-person perspective that (with one exception) is intimately introspective: therein lies an essential feature of his new musical persona.[73] "Remarkable how close in feeling Fechner is to Rückert," Mahler later observed; "they are two nearly related people and one side of my nature is linked with them as a third."[74] Like Fechner, the universalist who regards the entire universe as an organic spiritual hierarchy leading up to the deity, Rückert, too, sees all-encompassing unity manifest in both the simplest aspects of existence and in the complex systems of languages and cultures; his projection of feeling into nature is much akin to both Fechner's and Mahler's. And for Rückert, dying in love leads to the realm of eternal light, a view much akin to Fechner's belief that death is but the transition to the third stage of being, that of eternal waking, in which man is merged as one with waves of light and sound.

Rückert was an orientalist whose immersion in Eastern literature strongly influenced his own poetry; meditative, mystical withdrawal from earthly hubbub was a familiar notion for him. It was for Mahler as well, both from childhood experiences and via Schopenhauer's notion of stilling the driving will, the "wheel of Ixion." Such is also the central theme of Rückert's poem "Ich bin der Welt abhanden gekommen [I have become lost to the world]," which inspired the most extraordinary song Mahler had yet composed: "It is my very self!" he told Natalie just after it was completed.[75] If less than superlative poetry, Rückert's lyrics were the perfect catalyst for Mahler, who believed that the text of a song "actually constitutes only a hint of the deeper content that is to be drawn out of it, of the treasure that is to be hauled up."[76] To bring forth this treasure, he drew heavily upon the anhemitonic ("without semitones") pentatonic scale, the most common mode of pitch organization in Eastern music, just as he would later in *Das Lied von der Erde*. Both the mild exoticism of the pentatonic scale and its capacity to diffuse goal-oriented Western tonal processes are extensively exploited in "Ich bin der Welt abhanden gekommen." Yet almost paradoxically, it is precisely the hybrid mixture of tonality and pentatonicism that infuses this piece with concentrated organic coherence such as Mahler had previously achieved only in certain passages of the Fourth Symphony. (And as noted above, the close of the Fourth's slow movement is the prototype for the conclusion of "Ich bin der Welt.") Following the second performance of the lied in 1905, Mahler emphasized his organic approach to composition in conversation with Schoenberg and young Anton von Webern:

Nature is for us the model in this realm. Just as in nature the entire universe has developed from the primeval cell, from plants, animals, and men beyond to God, the Supreme Being, so also in music should a larger structure develop from a single motive in which is contained the germ of everything that is yet to be.[77]

Additional notable features of "Ich bin der Welt" and other Rückert settings of 1901 include subtle suppleness of line, delicacy of texture occasionally blurred by heterophony, and, in the orchestral versions, instrumentation that frequently borders on chamber music. All of the characteristics just reviewed – personal perspective, pentatonic exoticism, organic unification from cell to whole, and subtlety of texture – become central aspects of *Das Lied von der Erde*. While it may be historiographically questionable to regard these Rückert lieder of 1901 as "preparing for *Das Lied*," their affinities to Mahler's later symphony for voices and orchestra can scarcely be overestimated.[78]

A third syzygial pair: the Fifth and Sixth Symphonies

Eternal recurrence? the Fifth Symphony

When Mahler married, his tireless chronicler Natalie was out of the picture, and Alma was not so interested as Natalie had been in preserving his utterances. Thus we have less direct information about the middle-period symphonies (Nos. 5 through 7). Yet notwithstanding Mahler's new stylistic phase at the turn of the century, "it is the same old composer who confronts us, and unmistakably the same personality," as Donald Mitchell wryly notes.[79] Accordingly, it is not difficult to grasp the broad import of the Fifth and Sixth Symphonies, another brace of paired opposites. Just as the Fourth takes high classical form as the backdrop for its individuality, the Fifth sidesteps traditional formats in its groupings of movements and, particularly, by eschewing the dialectical conflict-and-resolution pattern of sonata form. Rather, all movements of the Fifth are rondo-like, and thereby proffer less the possibility of transcendence than the likelihood that their distinctive refrains and interrelated couplets may cycle on endlessly – rather like the Nietzschean eternal recurrence of all woe and all joy. The Fifth spirals gradually and uncertainly from funereal gloom and bitter irony in its closely intertwined first

two movements (C♯ minor and A minor respectively), through boundless driving energy in the D major scherzo (still darkly tinged at times),
to an interlude of intimate rapture in the famous Adagietto (F major), to
a D major finale of heady, boisterous, yet inconclusive joy. Here again (as
the autograph score confirms), Mahler structured the symphony in
Abteilungen: (I) the thematically related funeral march and second movement; (II) the scherzo; and (III) Adagietto plus Rondo–Finale, also thematically (and ironically) intertwined.

The Fifth's scherzo is a quantum leap in energy and radiance. It is also
the single movement for which we have commentary from Mahler,
revealing that its inspiration is markedly Nietzschean. A preliminary
plan for the Fourth Symphony (from 1895–96) lists the title "Die Welt
ohne Schwere – D-dur (Scherzo)," yet there is no such movement in the
Fourth as we know it. However, "The world without cares," or perhaps
better translated "without gravity," certainly fits the Fifth's scherzo;[80] as
Mahler told Natalie in the summer of 1901,

> "Every note is charged with life, and the whole thing whirls around in a
> giddy dance." He also compared it to a comet's tail: ". . . it is simply the
> expression of exorbitant energy. It is a human being in the full light of day,
> in the prime of his life."[81]

Later he offered Alma a slightly different description:

> oh heavens, what are they to make of this chaos that eternally gives birth to
> a new world, which perishes again in the next moment – of these primeval
> sounds, this foaming, roaring, raging sea, of these dancing stars, of these
> breath-taking, iridescent, flashing breakers?[82]

This is the language of Nietzsche, whose *Fröhliche Wissenschaft* extols
"'light feet,' 'dancing,' 'laughter' – and ridicule of 'the spirit of
gravity.'"[83] And Zarathustra exhorts:

> Come, let us kill the spirit of gravity [*Geist der Schwere*] . . . Now I am
> light, now I fly, now I see myself beneath myself, now a god dances
> through me . . .

> I say unto you: one must still have chaos in oneself to be able to give
> birth to a dancing star. I say unto you: you still have chaos in your-
> selves.[84]

Such is the nature of the "exorbitant energy" that ultimately prevails in
this extraordinary movement, which, in its admixture of Viennese waltz

and quasi-fugal learned counterpoint, is among the most complex pieces Mahler had yet written. The scherzo is the pivot from grimness to brightness in the Fifth.

Initially the symphony was to comprise the traditional four movements, all independent and self-contained. That plan, like much in Mahler's life, changed when he discovered Alma. Although he had not attempted to compose during the hurly-burly opera season for over a dozen years, during the winter of 1901–02, according to credible evidence, he penned the Fifth's Adagietto as a declaration of love for his bride-to-be.[85] Laced with appoggiaturas as well as allusions to the "glance" motive that inevitably recall *Tristan*, the Adagietto concludes with the meditative passage that closes both the Fourth Symphony's slow movement and "Ich bin der Welt abhanden gekommen"; in the latter the text is "Ich leb' allein in meinem Himmel, in meinem Lieben, in meinem Lied [I live alone in my heaven, in my love, in my song]." But in the Adagietto, music that had been deathly serene – "gänzlich ersterbend" in the Fourth, "Innig . . . pp . . . ohne Steigerung [intimate, pianissimo, without intensification]" in the song – has become passionately ecstatic: "*ff breit viel Ton!* Drängend [fortissimo, broad, lots of tone! Urgently]." Indeed, it is the climax of the piece.

The clue to this ostensible paradox lies in the Adagietto's allusions to *Tristan*, Wagner's musical manifestation of the Schopenhauerian worldview. The love-death dialectic is of course fundamental to *Tristan und Isolde*, and during the second-act love duet they commit themselves to "lovely Death, yearningly desired death in love! [*sehnend verlangter Liebes-Tod!*]" – a consummation achieved only through Isolde's Transfiguration at the conclusion of the work. According to Schopenhauer, Eros and Thanatos are syzygial opposites, holding the balance as mutual conditions of each other; Shiva bears both the necklace of skulls and the *lingam*. Mahler's fervent hope was to unite "his very self" with the stunningly beautiful twenty-three-year-old musician, in love, song, and eternal destiny. As we shall see, the love-death dynamic reemerges in *Das Lied von der Erde*, and again in the context of music "lost to the world."

The Fifth's Rondo-Finale, as noted, is joyous yet curiously inconclusive, and something of a pot-pourri, its virtuosity notwithstanding. The scherzo's learned counterpoint is revived, almost tongue-in-cheek; the Adagietto theme assumes an unexpected up-beat swing that seems almost cruelly parodistic; and Mahler weaves in bits of his sardonically

witty *Wunderhorn* song "Lob der Kritik [In praise of Lofty Understand-
ing]" about the singing contest between a cuckoo and a nightingale,
adjudicated by an ass. At length the chorale foreshadowed in the symphony's second movement emerges in full shimmer, but it has nothing
like the affirmative power of, say, the "Resurrection" chorale in the
Second Symphony. Gerlach suggests the Fifth's conclusion is but one in
a series of artistic usurpations inspired by Nietzsche, whereby the topos
of the chorale is appropriated to celebrate the *Übermensch* in a world
without God.[86] According to Zarathustra, prophet of the *Übermensch*,
eternal recurrence means that saying yes to a single joy is saying yes to all
woe as well: "All things are entangled, ensnared, enamored; if ever you
wanted one thing twice, if you ever said 'You please me, happiness!
Abide, moment!' then you wanted *all* back."[87] And the finale to the first
three parts of *Zarathustra*, "The Seven Seals" (published well before
part 4), is itself a rondo, repeatedly punctuated by the refrain, "Oh, how
should I not lust after eternity and after the nuptial ring of rings, the ring
of recurrence . . . *For I love you, O eternity!*"[88] Such a reading of Mahler's
finale would explain, at least in part, its ambivalent, often flippant entan-
gling of the quotidian with symbols of inconclusive transcendence. In
any case, as de La Grange observes, in the Fifth Mahler goes further than
hitherto "in instinctively assuming the uncertainty, the doubts, the
secret anguish, the fundamental ambiguity, that marked his time and still
weigh so heavily on ours."[89] It is hardly coincidental that he would write
such a work in 1901–02.

Tragedy immutable: the Sixth Symphony

The subtitle of the Sixth, "Tragic," is Mahler's own, as is the well-
known précis of its finale: "It is the hero, on whom fall three blows of fate,
the last of which fells him as a tree is felled."[90] Not only the conclusion,
but the overall structure differs fundamentally from the Fifth's: there are
four movements of traditional stamp, and the dialectic of sonata form is
utterly central to the first and last. It is as though the condensed classi-
cism of the celestial Fourth were inverted and expanded into a tragic
vision ending in a nihilistic void. All but the Sixth's slow movement are
in A minor, the key of the Fifth's wildly agitated second movement,
which would become one of two principal tonalities in *Das Lied von der
Erde*.

24

Mahler is at the height of his powers as symphonic dramatist in the Sixth, and its dark outcome is by no means certain until the recapitulation in the finale. The opening Allegro, dominated by the relentless tread of the military march, is as tightly constructed as any symphonic first movement since Beethoven (the "Eroica" was probably Mahler's prototype here); the dynamic interplay between ominous and joyous material is carefully balanced throughout, and the resulting momentum sweeps beyond the boundaries of traditional form without obliterating it. The scherzo fuses elements of the march, waltz, and Ländler into a complex and horrific dance of death, mitigated by folkish trio sections Mahler associated with the arrhythmic playing of his two little children staggering through the sand.[91] The Andante, Mahler's first full-scale symphonic slow movement (the finale of the Third is a special case), is suffused with nostalgia; the words from the first of the *Kindertotenlieder* echoed in the principal theme reveal one aspect of its longing: "as though no misfortune had transpired in the night . . ." (The same phrase is prominently cited very near the end of *Das Lied*.) But in the finale, as in Nietzsche's account of *The Birth of Tragedy*, the terrors of individual existence and its sorrowful end pierce us just at those moments when, in Dionysian ecstasy, we anticipate the indestructibility and eternity of infinite primordial joy.[92] The dramatic irony here is that *we* know well in advance what outcome fate and form will demand; yet the music, the direct manifestation of will, courses on as though oblivious.[93] The final devastation is as complete and overwhelming as that of *King Lear*.

The Seventh and Eighth Symphonies

"Was kost' die Welt?": ironic ambivalence in the Seventh Symphony

Mahler's Seventh has remained his most perplexing work, from its premiere to the present day. The seeming lack of overall relation or progression from movement to movement and the uproariously "cheerful" tone of its highly disjunct finale are quite the opposite of the Sixth's tight construction and black conclusion. From Mahler's scanty hints and the character of the music itself, we can gather that the three inner movements are nocturnal vignettes – of a patrol watch, a nightmare, and a romantic serenade in a style that Alma Mahler characterized as "Eichendorff-ish."[94] The outer members of this trilogy, the two *Nachtmusiken*, both evoke the sort of immediate life reflected in the medium of memory that Adorno identifies as central to Mahler's late style, particularly in the inner movements of *Das Lied von der Erde*. The Seventh's scherzo, like the opening movements of the Fifth, reminds us once again how strongly certain passages in Mahler already adumbrate the anguished, distorted musical language of Expressionism, as will the opening "Drinking Song of Earth's Sorrow" in *Das Lied*. And the first movement of the symphony contains a new twist on traditional tonal language: constellations of motivic fourths give rise to frequent added-sixth and half-diminished-seventh sonorities, anticipating Schoenberg's later use of quartal harmony.[95] Such exotic fusion of horizontal and vertical dimensions in music is a further outgrowth of Mahler's pentatonic organicism in "Ich bin der Welt abhanden gekommen," and the technique would soon assume paramount importance in *Das Lied von der Erde*.

But the finale, relentlessly discursive and chock-full of allusions to other music, remains ironically ambivalent up through its famous concluding cadence. The corresponding movement of the Fifth is its closest relation; still, the Seventh's concluding irony is different in tone from anything else in Mahler – as striking as his purported flippant summation of the movement: "Was kost' die Welt? [What is the world worth?]"[96] Perhaps he had already anticipated the endlessly overlapping circles of irony characteristic of post-modernity.

Faustian redemption? the Eighth

"The negative import of the Sixth had been explicit," writes de La Grange. "That of the Seventh is implicit. Here Mahler has arrived at an extreme position, a point of no return after which it was absolutely necessary for him to change course."[97] The result was the monumental Eighth, feverishly composed in the single summer of 1906, "as if it had been dictated to me."[98] In a now-famous letter to the conductor Willem Mengelberg he declared:

> I have just finished my Eighth. – It is the grandest thing I have yet done. – And so peculiar in content and form that it is really impossible to write anything about it. Try to imagine the whole universe beginning to ring and resound. These are no longer human voices, but planets and suns revolving.[99]

26

The theme of salvation through Faustian striving is evident in Mahler's work from the time of the First and Second Symphonies, and he had long hoped to set the conclusion of Goethe's venerated masterwork. But its unlikely coupling with the ancient Latin hymn "Veni Creator Spiritus" had struck Mahler like a lightning bolt. The bridge between them, he told Webern, was the passage "accende lumen sensibus . . . [enkindle light in our senses, pour love into our hearts]"[100] – a return to his oft-repeated belief in the unity of God and love. As we shall see, the large bipartite scheme of this work would also prove influential upon *Das Lied von der Erde*.

As Mahler's dithyramb to Mengelberg indicates, the Eighth is not easily summed up. No other secular work of music has made more powerful claims to cosmic grandeur and significance; the sheer massiveness of its optimistic utterance is astounding. At the time of its completion, Mahler considered the work "a gift to the nation" and believed that

> All my earlier symphonies are only preludes to this one. In the other works everything is subjectively tragic – this one is a great bestower of joy.[101]

Yet within a year he would abandon that mode of writing forever. In the wake of what took place in 1907, Mahler moved even farther from grandeur toward intimacy than he had between the Third and Fourth Symphonies. Stylistically, he resumed paths first explored after his near-fatal collapse in 1901.

2

Genesis

The events of 1907

Mahler's directorship of the Vienna Court Opera had always been surrounded by tension. Uncompromising in the pursuit of his ideals, Mahler was always prepared to resign his position should it prove necessary to play the last card in asserting his authority. He had achieved much in nine years, most notably in legendary new productions of Wagner, Mozart, and Beethoven in collaboration with his chosen scenic adviser, the Secessionist artist Alfred Roller. He had also weathered innumerable scandals, intrigues, criticisms, and resentments. And reluctantly, Mahler had become resigned to the realities of repertory theater: an institution such as the Court Opera, which was engaged in the business of presenting different works on a daily basis, could never consistently maintain his standards, which were those of a festival consecrated to the highest level of performance. Within a month of announcing the completion of his Eighth Symphony, he complained bitterly to Willem Mengelberg of "this damned theatrical turmoil, which I won't be able to bear much longer . . .," and he had hinted of his departure from the Opera in conversation with a critic earlier that summer.[1]

During these years Mahler's fame as a composer was gradually growing, which meant travels away from Vienna to conduct his works. Certain Viennese critics who were ever alert to the possibility of a scandal and the opportunity to attack the director had begun to claim, without justification, that Mahler's absences were adversely affecting both the quality of performances and the box-office revenues. Mahler, meanwhile, long dissatisfied with the antiquated style of ballet performance at the Opera, gave his approval in February of 1907 to Alfred Roller's secret selection and coaching of an unknown young dancer for the role of Fenella in *La muette de Portici*, all of which was in defiance of

28

the official ballet master, Hassreiter. This administrative irregularity, the first he had ever committed, brought Mahler a reprimand from the Opera's royal intendant, Prince Montenuovo. Another collision with authority involved Mahler's plan to prolong his Easter vacation to conduct concerts in Italy that year. Rumors of all sorts appeared in the press. Mahler illustrated his situation for Bruno Walter by grasping a chair and tilting its legs: "You see, that's what they are doing to me: if I wanted to remain seated, all I would have to do is to lean back firmly and I could hold my place. But I am not offering any resistance, and so I shall finally slide off."[2] The terms of Mahler's departure were agreed upon in March, and by mid-May he was seriously negotiating for a position at the Metropolitan Opera in New York that would provide him with five times his previous salary for a working season of only three months. Nevertheless, quitting the Vienna Opera evidently bothered Mahler more than he wished to let on, and according to Alma he became nervous, irritable, and moody.[3] To his friend the physicist Arnold Berliner he wrote in mid-June: "It is all quite true. I am going because I can no longer endure the rabble."[4]

At the end of June Mahler and his family retreated as usual to their summer villa at Maiernigg on the Wörthersee. Within days the older of the two girls, Maria, had contracted scarlet fever; she died within a fortnight. Named after Mahler's adored mother, little Maria had been his favorite, "his child entirely" according to Alma. The girl was accustomed to visit her father's studio every morning, where they held long conversations, the subject of which no one else ever knew; she usually emerged covered with jam, to the consternation of the nurse. "[T]hey were so happy together after their talk . . .," Alma reports. Understandably, Mahler was utterly devastated by her death. The depth of his attachment to Maria is revealed by his wish to be buried in her grave, as in fact he was.[5] This was the second blow of the year; the third soon followed.

Maria's death left Alma "suffering from extreme exhaustion of the heart." The local doctor was summoned, and he also examined Mahler: "Well, you've no cause to be proud of a heart like that," was his verdict. Both Mahler's mother and his younger brother Ernst had suffered heart disease; he immediately consulted a specialist in Vienna, who confirmed the diagnosis of valvular defect. As was customary at the time, Mahler, for whom bicycling, swimming, and mountain climbing had been essential summer exercise, was ordered to greatly restrict his physical activities.[6] The family fled from Maiernigg to a hotel in Schluderbach, near Toblach, in the area of the Tyrol where Mahler would spend the remainder of his summer composing holidays.

According to Alma, the summer's sad events "marked the beginning of the end for Mahler," but recent writers have questioned how seriously all of this affected him and his late music. To be sure, it now seems that Alma's accounts somewhat exaggerate Mahler's physical and psychological frailty between the summer of 1907 and the crisis of her affair with Walter Gropius in 1910 – precisely to justify her involvement with a lover, which was the greatest shock of Mahler's life.[7] But we have accounts other than Alma's: Alfred Roller, who visited the Mahlers in Schluderbach that summer, reports that the effect of the heart diagnosis upon Mahler was "severe and disabling . . . His mood was one of silent resignation."[8] In mid-September Bruno Walter wrote his parents of Mahler's despair over the death of his daughter: "He is completely broken up from it; outwardly no one can tell, but whoever knows him well realizes that inwardly he is completely finished [*ganz fertig*]."[9] And Mahler's two letters to Walter from the summer of 1908 (cited below, pp. 33–34) are moving testimony of the trials he was facing during this period. Thus, regardless of how one reads Mahler's Ninth Symphony, his last completed score, there can be little doubt that its predecessor *Das Lied von der Erde* was a creation *sub specie mortis*; as Bruno Walter summed it up, "Death, towards whose mysteries his thought and perception had so often taken their flight, had suddenly come in sight."[10]

We do not know exactly what Mahler's physicians told him about his heart condition. But it had long been known that there was a connection between faulty heart valves and malignant endocarditis – strings of microbes growing from the damaged valves – which was invariably fatal prior to the discovery of antibiotics. At the turn of the century Viennese medical knowledge was among the most advanced in the world, and the German cardiologist Theodor von Jürgensen published in Vienna detailed studies of cardiac weakness, endocarditis, and valvular deficiencies between 1899 and 1903. From these it emerges that overtaxing a weakened heart was considered very dangerous; thus it is not surprising that Mahler was advised to restrict his activities. According to Jürgensen, no one could predict when complications from faulty heart valves might arise: some patients could survive mild valvular defects for several years without serious difficulty, only to die quickly from endocarditis. Jürgensen particularly warns against the dangers of colds and respiratory infections that could lead to the more serious disease. But to worry the patient unduly seems unwarranted in his view. Accordingly, he cites with approval the advice of another cardiologist, von Leyden: "One should not tell the heart patient the whole truth, but one may not conceal from him that he has to regulate his mode of life appropriately." And he continues:

> Thus one should remain silent about the menacing danger of a recurring endocarditis, because one simply does not know oneself whether it will occur at all, or when, any more than one knows how to avoid it. But that a heart with valvular ailment must be protected from fatigue has to be said to the person suffering from it.[11]

Mahler's devastation in the wake of his doctors' diagnosis suggests that one of them may well have revealed the serious dangers of endocarditis (from which he eventually died in 1911). And it would be characteristic of Mahler to ask for the truth: he faced his brush with death in 1901 stoically, and at the onset of his final illness he insisted on knowing whether it would be fatal.[12]

Composition: chronology and chronicle

Alma Mahler suggests that the composition of *Das Lied von der Erde* began in the summer of 1907 during "long, lonely walks" in Schluderbach, after "an old consumptive friend of my father's" had given Mahler Hans Bethge's anthology *Die chinesische Flöte*, the source of the work's poetry.[13] But this chronology now appears inaccurate: the *Börsenblatt für den Deutschen Buchhandel*, a periodical that rigorously monitored new publications in Germany, states that the Bethge volume was first published on 5 October 1907, well after Mahler had left Schluderbach on 24 August.[14] According to Roller,

> That summer [1907] yielded no artistic fruit . . . in the summer of 1908 . . . his creative drive returned. Apparently to his own surprise: "Just think, I'm writing something again," he called out to me as I arrived. It was *Das Lied von der Erde*.[15]

Of the surviving manuscripts for the work, all that bear dates are from 1908 (see Table 2 below).

New York

In the intervening months Mahler had made his first venture to America, having bid farewell to the Viennese public with performances of *Fidelio* and his own Second Symphony, and having taken leave of friends and supporters at a surprise sendoff from the Westbahnhof on 9 December 1907. As the train pulled out, the painter Gustav Klimt, quoting the chorus at the moment of Faust's death, summed up the mood on the platform in a single word: "Vorbei! [It's all over!]" Fearing the voyage, Mahler "endeavored to avoid sea-sickness by lying rigidly on his back on his bunk like a cardinal on his tomb"[16] – he himself had used the same imagery to convey the serenity of the dead in describing the slow movement of his Fourth Symphony.[17] Mahler had often diverted himself from sorrow through hard work, and so he did in New York, although he now recognized the necessity of avoiding excessive fatigue, and therefore resolutely refused the offer of the Metropolitan Opera board to become director of the house. A month after his debut at the Met, Mahler wrote his father-in-law Carl Moll that he regarded America as "an awkward youth, whose incivilities one gladly overlooks as excesses of a driving force," yet found it refreshing "after the Viennese wilderness – to find sympathy and thanks everywhere for the little bit that I am able to contribute."[18] And he tried to persuade his colleagues Roller and Mengelberg to join him in the artistic life of the New World.[19] But Mahler was also lonely: "My homesickness, which has plagued me the whole time (unfortunately I remain an inveterate Viennese), is transforming itself into that certain excited longing, which you, too, surely know," he wrote a friend in April 1908, shortly before leaving New York for the summer.[20]

The summer of 1908

Although the Mahlers arrived back in Europe on 2 May, they did not make their way to Toblach until 11 or 12 June; concerts and visits intervened. Once ensconced in the Tyrol, Mahler had great difficulty getting to work. At first "for a long time . . . things were extremely unsettled *chez nous* and the spree of gaiety seemed to be declared permanent; then bouts of angina [= pharyngitis] and general nervousness crystallized, etc., etc."[21] Two poignant letters to Bruno Walter reveal that Mahler realized his tactics of diversion could no longer be maintained, and that he was forced to confront himself:

> I've mainly been trying to settle in here. This time I must change not only location, but my entire manner of living. You can imagine how difficult the latter is for me. For years I had been used to persistent and vigorous exercise. To wander around in mountains and forests, and to carry away my sketches from them in a kind of insolent robbery. I went to the desk only as a peasant goes to the barn: to give form to my sketches. Moreover, spiritual indispositions retreated after a hearty march (especially uphill). – Now I am supposed to avoid every exertion, monitor myself constantly, not walk much. At the same time in this solitude, where I am inwardly aware, I feel all the more clearly what is not in order in my physical being. Perhaps my outlook is altogether too black – but I feel worse since coming to the country than I did in the city, where distraction deceptively covered over much. – So I can't report much that's cheerful to you, and for the first time in my life I wish my vacation was over. It is fabulous here; if only once in my life I could enjoy such things after the completion of a work! For that, as you yourself will know, is the only moment in which one is truly capable of enjoyment. At the same time I have made a curious observation. I can do nothing but work; over the course of the years I have forgotten how to do anything else. It's as though I were a morphine addict or a drunkard to whom one forbade his vice all at once. I am making use of the sole virtue remaining to me: patience! Very likely I have chosen to be alone at exactly the wrong time. In such a frame of mind one is of course directed to the entertainments that come to one from without. And therefore I can only deeply regret the closing of the opera season, which now cuts off the main source of my amusements. – The latest Don Quixote prank is precious. What a shame that one can't come to know the details. For now, only best wishes, also from my wife . . .[22]

Bruno Walter suggested Mahler read *Zur Diätetik der Seele* (*Dietetics of the Soul*) by the Viennese physician Ernst von Feuchtersleben (1806–49), a small volume that promotes self-healing through self-mastery and identifies fear, especially of death, as the root of hypochondria. Walter had read it in 1906 while a patient of Sigmund Freud's, whose help he had sought to overcome a mysterious (and almost surely psychosomatic) paralysis of the arm that had made him unable to conduct. Walter also recommended that Mahler take a Scandinavian vacation, much as Freud had prescribed to Walter the rather unorthodox cure of an immediate trip to Sicily.[23] But Mahler rejected such solutions:

> But I can only come to myself and become conscious of myself here in solitude. – For ever since that panic terror I felt that time, I have tried to do nothing other than to look away and avert my ears. – If I am to find the way back to my self, then I must give myself up to the horrors of loneliness. But basically I am still only speaking in riddles, for you do not know what transpired and is transpiring in me; but it's not at all that hypochondriac fear of death, as you imagine. I already realized previously that I shall have to die. – But, without here trying to explain or describe to you something for which there are perhaps no words at all, I shall only tell you that quite simply at a stroke I lost all the clarity and reassurance that I ever achieved; and that I stood vis-à-vis de rien [face to face with nothing] and now at the end of a life I must learn to walk and stand as a beginner. – Is that a spiritual disposition that must be fought with a psychiatrist's weapons, as you believe? And as regards my "work," it is also somewhat depressing first to have to unlearn things. I can't work at a desk. For my inner activity I need outer activity. – What you're telling me about the doctors doesn't do me any good. An ordinary moderate march gives me such quickening of pulse and anxiety that I never achieve the goal of walking: to forget one's body. – During these days I read Goethe's letters. – His secretary, to whom he was accustomed to dictate correspondence, fell ill; this was such a disruption for him that he had to break off work in the midst of things for four weeks. – Just think about what it would be like for Beethoven if his legs were amputated as the result of an accident. If you know his way of living – do you think that he could right away have sketched even one movement of a quartet? And that doesn't compare well with my situation. I confess – superficial though it seems – this is the greatest calamity that has ever befallen me. I must absolutely begin a new life – and in that I am also a complete beginner.
>
> But now, so as not to close so tearfully, I will assure you that I have been relatively successful in coming to enjoy myself and life. And also that physically, on the whole, I am not doing badly. It is wonderful here . . . Enjoy a beautiful summer, and go walking (for me, too)! You don't at all know how beautiful that is.[24]

This second letter, dated 18 July, certainly suggests that Mahler was still making no headway composing that summer. "That panic terror" has never been specifically identified, but we know Mahler was so over-wrought at the time that he could easily fall from intense concentration into a state of anxiety. As always, he left orders that he was never to be disturbed while at work in the *Häuschen*. Nevertheless, one day an American piano salesman found his retreat and shouted at the top of his voice "How do you do?" Alma reports that Mahler sent the man packing and staggered back into the composing hut, where he suffered a heart spasm (*Herzkrampf*). "He came to me sobbing. He said he'd felt as though he had been thrown from the steeple of St. Stephen's Cathedral down to the pavement."[25] On another occasion, Bruno Walter tells us,

> he was suddenly frightened by an indefinable noise. All at once, "some-thing terribly dark" came rushing through the window and, when he jumped up in horror, he saw that he was in the presence of an eagle which filled the little room with its violence. The fearsome meeting was quickly over and the eagle disappeared as stormily as it had come. When Mahler sat down, exhausted by his fright, a crow came fluttering from under the sofa and flew out. The peaceful abode of musical absorption had become a battle-ground upon which one of the innumerable fights of "all against all" had taken place. Mahler's account of it still tingled with the horror of so striking a demonstration of the cruelty of nature which had ever been one of the reasons for his deep world-sorrow [*Weltschmerz*].[26]

The earliest date in any of the manuscripts for *Das Lied* – "Toblach Juli 1908" – appears at the end of the second song, which then still bore Bethge's original title: "Die Einsame im Herbst [The Lonely Woman in Autumn]" (see below, Table 2 and Plate 2; Mahler later made the song's persona masculine, *der Einsame*). Astonishingly, once underway, the symphonic cycle of six movements mushroomed in six weeks' time, apparently in the movement order 2–3–1–4–6 (there is no date for no. 5). Alma describes the process as follows:

> He worked feverishly the entire summer on the orchestral lieder with Chinese poems translated by Hans Bethge as texts. The work expanded in scale under his hands. He united the individual texts, composed inter-ludes, and the expanded forms continually drew him closer to his funda-

mental form – the symphony. When it was clear to him that this was again a sort of symphony, the work quickly took on form and was finished sooner than he believed it would be.[27]

The orchestral draft of "Der Abschied" is inscribed "1. September 1908," and shortly thereafter Mahler left Toblach for Prague, where the Seventh Symphony was to be premiered on September 19. He stopped briefly in Vienna, and announced his arrival there in a note to Bruno Walter:

> I was very diligent (from which you can gather that I've fairly well "gotten used to things"). I myself do not know how to express what the whole thing might be called. A beautiful time was granted me, and I believe it is the most personal thing I have yet created. Perhaps more about that in conversation . . . (I have to be diligent down to the last day in order to finish.)[28]

Thus, although more precise chronology is lacking, it would appear that *Das Lied von der Erde* began with Mahler's personal confrontation and transformation of his autumnal loneliness in "Die Einsame im Herbst." As was so often the case in previous years, "only when I experience do I 'compose,' and only when I compose do I experience!"

The texts

It seems curious that in the summer of 1908 Mahler should have found texts so well suited to his purpose in poems from the eighth-century Chinese T'ang dynasty. But the poems in Hans Bethge's *Die chinesische Flöte* are by no means literal or scholarly translations from Chinese; rather, they are *Nachdichtungen*, as Bethge calls them – "paraphrase poems" – which are thrice removed from original sources. No sinologist himself, Bethge worked chiefly from a German anthology by Hans Heilmann, which in turn is based on two French translations, by Le Marquis d'Hervey de Saint-Denys and Judith Gautier respectively.[29] Chinese poetry translated literally has, to Western ears, an atmospheric, sometimes almost telegraphic quality; thus, part of the problem of rendering such verse into a European language is to provide connectives of the sort readers of Chinese assume, and to make it seem less unusual to the

Western reader. Table 1 illustrates the process of transformation for the fifth poem in *Das Lied*, "Der Trunkene im Frühling [The Drunk in Spring]": the first column is a literal translation of the Chinese by Peter Yang; then follow the French version by d'Hervey de Saint-Denys, the German translation by Heilmann, and Bethge's *Nachdichtung*. Mahler's additional retouchings, which are minimal in this case, are underlined in the Appendix to this volume.[30]

As the table shows, Bethge adds more than just syntactical continuity. A literary figure of some standing during the first third of the century, Bethge wrote original poetry, novellas, stories, and essays, as well as several volumes of paraphrase poetry from various Eastern languages. As he observes in the foreword to one of these anthologies, "The point is not to translate a poem literally, but rather to reconstitute to a certain extent the spirit, the style, the melody of a poem in a foreign language."[31] *Die chinesische Flöte* was his first venture of this sort, and his afterword to that volume plainly reveals his Romantic passion. Of Li-Po, the principal poet in the collection, he writes:

> He turns into poetry the volatile, wind-swept, unutterable beauty of the world, the eternal sadness and enigma of all being. All the gloomy melancholy of the world took root in his breast, and even in moments of greatest joy he cannot free himself from the shadows of the earth. "Transitoriness" is the constantly admonishing stamp of his feeling.[32]

Such words might well characterize Mahler's setting of the Li-Po/Bethge "Das Trinklied vom Jammer der Erde" that opens *Das Lied von der Erde* (and indeed, after coming to know the work, Bethge wrote of it in similar terms).[33] But they also reveal how *Die chinesische Flöte* came to resemble German Romantic poetry with oriental overtones. Bethge's versification expands and vitalizes the delicately disjunct and seemingly timeless imagery of the ancient Chinese poets, and it accentuates the personal responses of the (usually nameless) protagonists. From this collection of eighty-three paraphrases of thirty-eight poets, Mahler selected seven verses, shaped them into an allegory of transitory existence merging into eternity, and gradually retouched them to serve his own expressive purposes.

Still, orientalism is central to *Das Lied*. From the days of Marco Polo

Table 1: *Four translations of the poem by Li-Po that became "Der Trunkene im Frühling"*

Literal English translation from the Chinese by Peter Yang (1999) "Rising from (in) drunkenness on a spring day, talking about ideal"	French translation by Le Marquis d'Hervey de Saint-Denys (Paris, 1862) "Un jour de printemps / le poète exprime ses sentiments au sortir de l'ivresse" ("A spring day; the poet expresses his feelings coming out of drunkenness")
Handling life is like a great dream	Si la vie est comme un grand songe, If life is like a big dream
Why should one worry about life	A quoi bon tourmenter son existence! What good [is it] to torment one's existence!
Therefore I am drunk all day	Pour moi je m'enivre tout le jour, For my part, I get drunk all day,
I fall suddenly before the main pillar	Et quand je viens à chanceler, je m'endors And when I start to stagger, I fall asleep au pied des premières colonnes.*a* at the foot of the first pillars.
When I am awake I see in front of the house	A mon réveil je jette les yeux devant moi; Upon awakening I cast a look before me;
A bird chirps among the flowers	Un oiseau chante au milieu des fleurs; A bird is singing amidst the flowers;

Je lui demande à quelle époque de l'année
I ask him what season of the year

nous sommes,
are we,

Il me répond à l'époque où le souffle
He answers me it's the season when the breath

du printemps fait chanter l'oiseau.
of spring makes the bird sing.

Je me sens ému et prêt a soupirer,
I feel moved and am ready to sigh,

Mais je me verse encore à boire;
But I pour myself something to drink again;

Je chante à haute voix jusqu'à ce que
I sing in a loud voice up to where

la lune brille,
the moon is shining,

Et à l'heure où finissent mes chants,
And at the time my songs are over,

j'ai de nouveau perdu
I've once again lost

le sentiment de ce qui m'entoure.
the feeling of what surrounds me.

I wonder what day it is

Spring wind talks like an oriole

I feel that I want to sigh

I pour the wine and drink it lonely

I am singing and waiting for the bright moon

When the songs are over everything is forgotten

Table 1 (*cont.*)

German translation by Hans Heilmann (Munich, 1905) "Ein Frühlingstag." ["A Spring Day"]	German translation by Hans Bethge (Leipzig, 1907) "Der Trinker im Frühling" ["The Drinker in Spring"]
	Wenn nur ein Traum das Dasein ist, If Being is only a dream,
Wenn das Leben ein Traum ist, If life is a dream,	
Warum sich mühen und plagen! Why trouble and torment oneself!	Warum dann Müh und Plag? Why then care and torment?
Ich, ich berausche mich den ganzen Tag Me, I get drunk all day	Ich trinke, bis ich nicht mehr kann, I drink until I can't anymore,
	Den ganzen lieben Tag. The whole loving day.
Und wenn ich zu schwanken beginne, dann sink' And when I begin to sway, then I fall	Und wenn ich nicht mehr trinken kann, And when I can't drink anymore,
ich vor der Tür meines Hauses zum before the door of my house into	Weil Leib und Kehle voll, Because body and throat are full,
	So tauml ich hin vor meiner Tür Then I stagger off to my door
Schlafe nieder. sleep again.	Und schlafe wundervoll! And sleep wonderfully!

Was hör ich beim Erwachen? Horch,
What do I hear upon awakening? Listen,

Ein Vogel singt im Baum.
A bird is singing in the tree.

Ich frag ihn, ob schon Frühling sei, –
I ask him whether it's already spring, –

Mir ist als wie im Traum.
It's as though I am in a dream.

Der Vogel zwitschert: ja, der Lenz
The bird twitters: yes, spring

Sei kommen über Nacht, –
arrived overnight, –

Ich seufze tief ergriffen auf,
I sigh, deeply moved,

Der Vogel singt und lacht.
The bird sings and laughs.

Wieder erwachend schlag ich die Augen auf.
Waking again, I cast my eyes about.

Ein Vogel singt in den blühenden Zweigen.
A bird is singing in the blossoming branches.

Ich frage ihn, in welcher Jahreszeit wir leben,
I ask him what season we're in,

Er sagt mir, in der Zeit, da der Hauch des
He says to me, in the time when the breath of

Frühlings den Vogel singen macht.
spring makes the birds sing.

Ich bin erschüttert, Seufzer schwellen mir die
I am shocked, sighs swell in my

Brust.
breast.

Table 1 (*cont.*)

German translation by Hans Heilmann (Munich, 1905) "Ein Frühlingstag." ["A Spring Day"]	German translation by Hans Bethge (Leipzig, 1907) "Der Trinker im Frühling" ["The Drinker in Spring"]
	Ich fülle mir den Becher neu I fill up my cup anew
Doch wieder gieß ich mir den Becher voll. Yet again I pour myself a full cup.	Und leer ihn bis zum Grund And empty it to the bottom
Mit lauter Stimme sing ich, bis der Mond With a loud voice I sing until the moon	Und singe bis der Mond erglänzt And sing until the moon glows forth
erglänzt. glows forth.	Am schwarzen Himmelsrund. In the dark sphere of the heavens.
Und wenn mein Sang erstirbt, hab ich auch And when my song dies away, I have also	Und wenn ich nicht mehr singen kann, And when I can't sing anymore,
wieder die Empfindung für die Welt um once again lost the perception of the world	So schlaf ich wieder ein. I go to sleep again.
mich verloren. around me.	Was geht denn mich der Frühling an! What do I care about spring!
	Laßt mich betrunken sein! Let me be drunk!

[a] This refers to the vestibule of Chinese houses (footnote by d'Hervey de Saint-Denis, condensed by SEH)

to the art of the Viennese Secession, Western interest in oriental culture had been both widespread and eclectic. Among poets whose work Mahler knew well, both Rückert and Goethe had composed collections of lyrics inspired by ancient Persian poetry; Goethe in his last years had turned again toward the East in his *Chinese-German Book of Hours and Seasons* (1827), a title that resonates with much of the poetic imagery Mahler adopted in *Das Lied*. Moreover, as we have seen, Mahler was from his youth steeped in Schopenhauer, whose call for the Buddhistic stilling of the will, "the veil of Maya," is liberally laced with allusions to classics of Eastern literature. Such meditative withdrawal from earthly hubbub is precisely what Mahler sought to compose into the Rückert song "Ich bin der Welt abhanden gekommen" shortly after his brush with death in 1901. Thus, spiritual transformation is one root of the orientalism in *Das Lied*.

Theodor Adorno, however, proposes a different view. He regards the work's "inauthentic Chinese element" as "a pseudomorph that does not take itself literally but grows eloquent through inauthenticity," embodying a "Romanticism of disillusionment" akin to that of Schubert's *Winterreise*, and related to Mahler's emigration. Moreover, for Adorno, who was Jewish, the stylized Orient of *Das Lied* is "pseudomorphous also as a cover for Mahler's Jewish element . . . by the euphemism of foreignness the outsider seeks to appease the shadow of terror."[34] Mahler's famous dictum of being thrice homeless – a Bohemian in Austria, an Austrian among Germans, and a Jew throughout the world – comes readily to mind in this context;[35] such considerations may also have drawn Mahler to the Bethge texts in the summer of 1908.

The stages of composition

Mahler's hesitation in naming his new creation probably stemmed from more than superstitious fear of "the Ninth." His short-score draft (German: *Particell*) of the final song, "Der Abschied," is labeled "Clavierauszug [piano version]," and the orchestral draft score of the third song specifies "Tenor or Soprano and Orchestra or Piano" (see Table 2 below). In fact, as he had done for all but one of his lieder from 1892 on, Mahler prepared a complete voice-and-piano version of this new work, eventually entitled *Das Lied von der Erde*, during its genesis. Evidently he began with the idea of writing songs, then perhaps a cycle; only gradually, as Alma tells us, did the symphonic scope of the whole emerge. To grasp this in perspective requires a brief review of Mahler's working methods.[36]

As his first letter to Walter cited above so touchingly underscores, Mahler was accustomed to compose only during the summer in the seclusion of the Austrian countryside, taking his sketches from nature "in a kind of insolent robbery." For this purpose he used pocket notebooks, of which only two have come down to us (neither pertaining to *Das Lied*). Then, "as a peasant goes to the barn," he returned to his composing hut (*Komponierhäuschen*) to work out his earlier ideas on full-size work sheets. The only such page known to survive for *Das Lied* is reproduced here as Plate 1. (Yet perhaps this is simply the first sketch of these bars, written of necessity at the desk owing to doctors' orders.) What happened next in the compositional process depended upon whether he was writing a song or a symphony. For symphonic works, Mahler proceeded toward the short score (*Particell*), a continuous ink draft on oblong paper scored in systems of three to five staves; although indications of instrumentation are sparse at this stage, both the essential continuity of the music and most of its textural detail are settled upon. Next came the orchestral draft score (*Partiturentwurf*), typically about twenty staves in oblong format, where Mahler worked out the essence of the orchestration. The foregoing were the fundamental steps of composition that, beginning in 1893, Mahler virtually always reserved for his summer working holiday, away from "the hellish life of the theatre";[37] the fair copy of the full orchestral score could be made by working a few hours each morning during the winter months. At that point the work was essentially finished, in that Mahler almost never altered the basic structure after the full score had been written. But he continued to revise details of orchestration and nuance almost every time he took up one of his scores – in the *Stichvorlage* (copyist's manuscript made for the engraver), in proof sheets, and both during and between rehearsals for a performance. (As he wrote to Bruno Walter in 1909, apparently in all seriousness, "I should like to publish new editions of my scores every 5 years..."[38])

Composing a song, however, was a more spontaneous, less arduous task; Mahler could write one in a day and orchestrate it the next. After

44

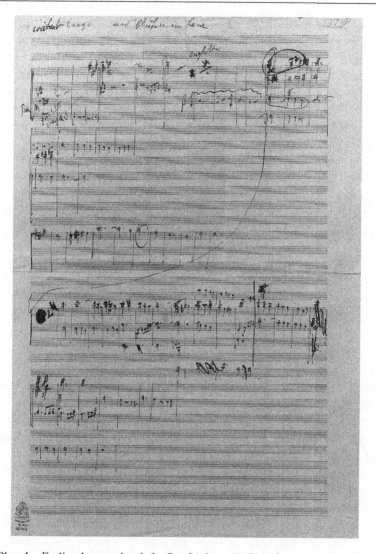

Plate 1   Earliest known sketch for *Das Lied von der Erde*, first mvt., related to
the opening of the development, fig. **25**–5 through **29**–5. The sketch shows a
signature of three sharps, indicating that Mahler originally planned this music
to sound a semitone higher (F♯/A) than it does in the final version.

preliminary sketching, he worked through one or more "quasi-pianistic" drafts, usually on three staves. Here, as in the symphonic *Particell,* he establishes both continuity and texture of the song, occasionally noting essential features of instrumentation, while elements of pianistic writing are also readily apparent. Thereby such a draft reflects Mahler's "dual-purpose" concept of the lied – for voice and either orchestra or piano. (And it is noteworthy that he himself occasionally performed his songs at the keyboard, even after the premiere of the orchestral version.[39]) Mahler next wrote the fair copy for voice and piano, and, to the best of our knowledge, proceeded directly to the fair copy of the full score without first making a preliminary orchestral draft. Thus, in writing lieder, the piano version effectively replaced the short-score stage of symphonic composition for Mahler. (*Stichvorlage* and revisions followed as in the symphonies.)

The unusual hybrid nature of *Das Lied von der Erde* is readily apparent from the autograph materials preserved from its composition, which are listed in Table 2. From these sources it emerges that the piano version did not replace the *Particell;* short scores survive for both the third and final movements (see, e. g., Plate 3 in chapter 4 below), and the piano version remained central to Mahler's conception of the work throughout the summer of 1908. Comparison of the manuscripts reveals that all movements of the keyboard setting were written before the fair copy of the orchestral score. Many details suggest that for movements 2 and 4, the piano version antedates the corresponding orchestral draft, while for movements 3 and 5, the order was probably the reverse (orchestral draft before piano version). But because Mahler frequently, although not consistently, incorporated the additions and revisions made in one of these manuscripts into the other, their chronology cannot be established with utter certainty. For the final movement, however, traces of the compositional process in the long instrumental interlude (fig. **36** ff.) clearly indicate that the orchestral draft of this section preceded the keyboard manuscript.

The orchestral draft of the finale is dated "1. September 1908," and Mahler left Toblach on September 4, probably just after completing the piano score, en route to rehearsals of the Seventh Symphony. Thus, he indeed worked diligently "down to the last day in order to finish," as he

Table 2: *The sources for Das Lied von der Erde*
Reproduced by kind permission of *The Journal of Musicology* from Stephen E.
Hefling, "*Das Lied von der Erde*: Mahler's Symphony for Voices and Orchestra
– or Piano," *Journal of Musicology* 10 (1992): 298–99.

Movement	Date	Description
1		Sketch page (= Plate 1).[a] One side, related to mm. 199–236 of the orchestral version, but from m. 203 on a half tone higher (F♯ minor instead of F minor). Piano Version[b]
	14. Aug. 1908	Orchestral Draft[c] (currently missing) Full Score[d]
2	Juli 1908	Piano Version[b] Orchestral Draft[e] (currently missing) Full Score[d]
3		Short Score[f] (Accolade: *Tenor / oder / Sopran / Clavier*) Piano Version[b] (Accolade: Sopr. oder / Tenor / Clavier)
	1. August 1908	Orchestral Draft[f] Full Score[d]
4	21. Aug. 1908	Piano Version[b] Orchestral Draft[d] Full Score[d]
5		Piano Version[b] Orchestral Draft[g] Full Score[d]
6		Short Score[h] (Title page: *Der Abschied / Clavierauszug / Mong-Kao-Jen / Wang-Wei*) Piano Version[b]
	1. September 1908	Orchestral Draft[h] Full Score[d]
All		*Stichvorlage;*[i] copyist unidentified. Contains autograph markings, but far fewer than usually encountered in such scores; also includes corrections by other

Table 2 (*cont.*)

Movement	Date	Description
		hands. Prepared for press by Josef Venantius von Wöss.

[a] Collection of Henry-Louis de La Grange, Bibliothèque Gustav Mahler, Paris; reproduced above as Plate 1.
[b] Private collection; published in *Gustav Mahler, Sämtliche Werke, kritische Gesamtausgabe*, Supplement Band II (Vienna, 1989), with photofacsimiles; photofacsimiles also in Hefling, "*Das Lied von der Erde*: Mahler's Symphony for Voices and Orchestra – or Piano," plates 1, 3, 4, and 5.
[c] Formerly in possession of Richard Specht; photofacsimiles (1) of the last page in *Moderne Welt*, Gustav Mahler Heft, III/7 (1921–22): 32; (2) of the title page and opening sheet of music, in Specht, *Gustav Mahler* (Berlin, 1913), plates 55 and 58, and also in *Die Musik* XIII/6 (1913), between pp. 368 and 369. The first page is also reproduced in Kurt Blaukopf, *Gustav Mahler oder der Zeitgenosse der Zukunft* (Vienna, 1969), 284; paperback edition (Kassel / Munich, 1973), 256.
[d] New York City, Pierpont Morgan Library, Robert Owen Lehman Deposit; photofacsimiles of the full score in Mitchell, *SSLD*, 172, 214, 250, 274, 312, and 338.
[e] Two pages are reproduced in Specht, *Gustav Mahler* (1913), plates 56 and 57.
[f] Vienna, Gesellschaft der Musikfreunde, A 315; photofacsimile, first page of the short score, in Kurt Blaukopf, comp. and ed., *Mahler: A Documentary Study* (New York, 1976), plate 284.
[g] Vienna, Stadt- und Landesbibliothek, MH 9482/c.
[h] The Hague, Gemeentemuseum, Willem Mengelberg Stichting; see Plate 3 below. Additional photofacsimiles in Rudolf Stephan, comp. and ed., *Gustav Mahler. Werk und Interpretation* (Cologne, 1979), 48–50; Hermann Danuser, *Gustav Mahler: Das Lied von der Erde*, Meisterwerke der Musik (Munich, 1986), facsimiles II and III following p. 139; and Mitchell, *SSLD*, 369, 375, 417, 421, 423, and 426.
[i] Vienna, Stadt- und Landesbibliothek, on loan from Universal Edition. See also Ernst Hilmar, "Mahleriana in der Wiener Stadt- und Landesbibliothek," *Nachrichten zur Mahler-Forschung*, no. 5 (June 1979): 7.

had written to Bruno Walter. Although the full score bears no dates, it was undoubtedly copied out during the fall and winter, as was Mahler's custom. While working on it he incorporated at least one notable revision in the first movement into both full score and piano version: an insert that provides the repetition of "ist mehr werth" in bars 163–66 (fig. 21 + 4 ff.). This indicates that the piano version remained central to Mahler's conception of *Das Lied* even as he was finishing the fair copy of the orchestral score. In the event, however, he did not carry out a thoroughgoing revision of his piano score, for reasons uncertain, as noted below.

The voice-and-piano autograph

Mahler's piano version remained unknown in private hands until its first publication in 1989 (*Kritische Gesamtausgabe*, Supplement Band II).[40] Two factors are essential to our understanding of this source. First, although on the whole a fair copy, it also represents a stage prior to the latest steps in the compositional process as outlined above; accordingly, there are numerous differences from the orchestral score. Second, *Das Lied* is the first of Mahler's compositions that he did not complete in his usual way – through performance, subsequent retouching, and overseeing the printing of the score. The three inner songs of the piano version are the clearest, and contain fewer variants than the more complex outer movements. Except for nos. 3 and 4, Mahler subsequently modified the poetic texts, and the keyboard manuscript itself reveals numerous instances of his touching up Bethge's version of the poetry. The titles of all but the opening movement were later changed as well. Every movement of the piano autograph includes differences from the orchestral score in pitch, accidentals, and precision of rhythmic notation. And characteristically, Mahler continually modified his performance indications (tempo, dynamics, phrasing and articulations, special nuances) throughout the gestation of the work.

Although there are perplexing discrepancies between the published piano and orchestral scores of Mahler's earlier songs (e.g., *Kindertotenlieder* and the other Rückert lieder), they are not nearly so extensive as those found in the manuscripts of *Das Lied*. Why Mahler did not revise and publish his own piano version remains something of a mystery. On 21 May 1910 he signed a contract with Universal Edition for the publication of both the Ninth Symphony and *Das Lied von der Erde*; thereby UE was "obliged to publish a piano reduction of each of the two works," and an insertion in Mahler's hand specifies "of the Song of the Earth a 2–hands [reduction] with text."[41] Very likely he knew that this task would be accomplished by Josef Venantius von Wöss, whose piano-vocal score of the Eighth Symphony pleased Mahler very much.[42] Perhaps lack of time prompted Mahler's decision to abandon his own piano version. He knew that his heart condition could shorten his life; his duties in New York were taxing, and he was making a serious effort to curb his habit of overworking. He had finished the Ninth Symphony,

Plate 2   "Die Einsame im Herbst," autograph version for voice and piano, final page, showing the earliest date found in any known manuscript of *Das Lied von der Erde* (first publication).

and intended to write another. Moreover, by May 1910 complex preparations were already underway for the colossal premiere of the Eighth Symphony the following September; Mahler was involved in these rehearsals through most of May and June. And it may be that he simply came to regard *Das Lied* as a more orchestral work than his earlier dual-purpose songs.

It is uncertain whether Wöss knew of Mahler's keyboard manuscript. In any case, his reduction, published by Universal in time for the 1911 orchestral premiere, differs greatly from the composer's version. Wöss attempted to transcribe all of the orchestral texture that could possibly be realized at the keyboard, whereas Mahler had sought to create not merely a reduction, but a setting for voices and piano well suited to the nature of the instrument. Thus, despite the complexity of the music in the short scores and orchestral drafts, Mahler did not hesitate occasionally to dispense with notable features of the texture to make it more idiomatic for the pianist. Thirty years after Wöss's arrangement appeared, UE issued a less complicated keyboard reduction by Erwin Stein, who may have known of Mahler's version.[43] If so, he made but little use of it, for his solutions to the problems of adapting this music for piano are notably less elegant than Mahler's.

In keeping with the policies of the Mahler Gesamtausgabe, the published volume of the autograph piano version corrects only obvious errors and omissions in the manuscript. But there is no reason why performers should not incorporate the various additions and alterations found in the orchestral sources to make the keyboard score congruent with Mahler's latest casting of the music. Accordingly, the critical report for the Gesamtausgabe keyboard version was prepared so as to facilitate such re-editing.

Editions of the orchestral score

As noted above, Mahler did not live to oversee the printing and first performances of *Das Lied von der Erde*; those tasks were entrusted to Bruno Walter. Mahler did see the *Stichvorlage* of the score, and made a few annotations in it; the bulk of the editing in that source, however, is of uncertain provenance, and may have come from Walter or employees of Universal Edition. The first edition (1912) was the principal source of the work until its publication in the Gesamtausgabe, edited by Erwin Ratz, in 1964; that edition was also reproduced as a Philharmonia miniature score (no. 217). Since then several scholars have raised questions about various readings, and in the course of preparing the piano version for the Gesamtausgabe all of the various sources were reviewed again. Following this, Karl Heinz Füssl, then general editor of the Gesamtausgabe, issued an improved version (*Verbesserte Ausgabe*) of the orchestral score (Vienna: Universal Edition, 1990) incorporating some, but not all, of the possible emendations performers may wish to consider.[44]

The question of the voice parts: alto or baritone?

Some of the preliminary manuscript sources for *Das Lied von der Erde* suggest that in the early stages of composition, Mahler was uncertain about the distribution of the vocal parts in the work. In both the *Particell* and the keyboard manuscript, for example, the third song (eventually entitled "Von der Jugend") is designated for either tenor or soprano. The keyboard autograph assigns the first song to the tenor, but indicates that the second is simply for "Singstimme [voice]," and leaves the vocal part unspecified in movements 4 through 6. But by the time of the orchestral full score, Mahler had clearly marked nos. 1, 3, and 5 for "Tenorstimme [tenor voice]," while 2, 4, and 6 were to be for "Alt-Solo," "Alt-St.[imme]," and "Alt" respectively – i.e., all for alto. Similarly, in a list of titles he drew up for the work at the Hotel Savoy in New York, probably during the 1909–10 season, the entire composition is at last entitled, perhaps for the first time, "Das Lied von der Erde / aus dem Alt-Chinesischen": here the second, fourth, and sixth movements are for "Alt."[45]

A single authentic source gives rise to the possibility of performing *Das Lied* with two male voices: in the *Stichvorlage*, at the first entrance of the "Alt-Stimme" in the second song, Mahler added the annotation: "(kann eventuell auch von Baryton übernommen werden [could possibly also be taken over by a baritone]." He did not, however, change the designations "Alt-Stimme" and "Alt" in movements 4 and 6 of the *Stichvorlage*. At the world premiere in 1911 Bruno Walter performed the work with tenor and alto; for the first Viennese performance the following year, however, he substituted the baritone Friedrich Weidemann, one of Mahler's favorite singers, for the alto soloist. In his autobiography

Walter notes that he never repeated the experiment because, although Weidemann gave his best, the demands of the part were better suited to the alto voice, which also provides welcome contrast.[46] Julius Korngold, principal critic of the *Neue freie Presse* who was among Mahler's solid supporters during his last years, found it "incomprehensible" that Mahler had considered the substitution of a baritone for the alto, and felt that the part lay too high for Weidemann; Alban Berg, too, reported to Schoenberg that "Weidemann was vocally inadequate."[47] Near the end of his life Bruno Walter reiterated his position on the matter:

> *Never again* . . . from then on [i.e., 1912] I have always used an alto voice . . . two male voices do the work no good. Mahler never heard Das Lied von der Erde – in my firm conviction, based on practical experience, he himself would have realized the error of giving the three songs to a baritone.[48]

And Otto Klemperer, who rarely agreed with Walter, came to the same conclusion: "I think a contralto is much better. Although Mahler himself suggested it, I find that the piece sounds monotonous with two men's voices, and God knows it isn't that."[49] Given that the publication of the work for either alto or baritone stems from a single provisional marking of Mahler's, the use of a baritone soloist seems dubious.

3

Reception

Overall, the reception history of *Das Lied von der Erde* is the same as that of Mahler's entire oeuvre.[1] Public acclaim of the "Resurrection" Symphony together with its positive assessment by a few critics had put Mahler the composer on the musical map of Europe in 1896; his appointment to the Vienna Court Opera the following year made his name all the more widely known. During the decade 1901–10 Mahler gave the premieres of his next six symphonies, plus *Das klagende Lied* and many of his orchestral lieder, to audiences generally divided into partisans and detractors. Only the Eighth Symphony was an overwhelming success, yet even then a number of the critics could not refrain from finding fault in Mahler's art.[2] His supporters included young people, especially youthful musicians, plus those of earlier generations sufficiently open-minded to take his often shocking innovations seriously. Among his detractors were antisemites – especially in Vienna, including a number of journalists – as well as conservative critics and listeners generally. And Mahler had offended a number of influential people either through his relentless pursuit of excellence over and against local politics at the Opera, or because he could not pretend to be submissive to the mediocre abilities and often self-serving schemes of the intelligentsia.

After Mahler's death, memorial concerts of his music were presented in numerous cities (Amsterdam, Berlin, Leipzig, Hamburg, Cologne, Vienna, etc.). It was on such a program in Munich that the premiere of *Das Lied von der Erde* took place (see below). Indeed, by the time *Das Lied* was first heard in Vienna (November 1912), Julius Korngold, principal critic of Vienna's *Neue freie Presse*, would venture to state that Mahler was perhaps the most frequently performed of modern composers on German concert programs during that season. A coterie of mostly young musicians (several of Jewish ancestry) continued to champion Mahler's works up to and after the First World War; among them were Schoenberg and his followers Berg, Webern, Heinrich Jalowetz, and Karl Horwitz; the conductors Bruno Walter, Willem Mengelberg, Otto Klemperer, Oskar Fried, and Artur Bodanzky; and the journalists and musicologists Richard Specht, Paul Stefan, Guido Adler, and Paul Bekker. Notwithstanding resistance in various quarters, Mahler's music was gradually making its way into the symphonic repertoire, especially in Germany and Austria. In the case of *Das Lied von der Erde*, for example, we know of at least seventeen performances that took place between 1911 and 1915, in Munich, Zurich, Leipzig, Frankfurt, Prague, Graz, Mannheim, Berlin, Vienna, Hamburg, Wiesbaden, Budapest, and Amsterdam.[3] A highpoint in the reception of Mahler's oeuvre was the nearly complete cycle presented by Mengelberg and the Concertgebouw in Amsterdam, from 6 through 21 May 1920. But beginning in 1933 all works by Jewish artists were banned from Germany by the Nazi regime, and also from Austria following the *Anschluß* in 1938; Mahler was not heard again in those countries until the end of the Second World War. Occasional performances took place in English-speaking lands, especially in the USA, whence many middle-European musicians had fled during the Nazi era. But only after the war did Mahler slowly reemerge in the concert repertoire and, significantly, on recordings, which were to be immensely beneficial to his rapidly growing popularity.

The Swiss critic William Ritter, whose reviews of *Das Lied* are summarized below, reveals that the work's premiere was indeed a microcosm of Mahler reception overall at the time:

> everything proceeded in accordance with the experience of the previous premieres. The same faithful followers, the same curiosities hastened from the four corners of the world, the same triumphal reception among the youth, the suffering, the disinherited of this world, the sincere and sensible, and the same disdainful condemnation among a portion of the critics, the loftily esteemed portion, those who belabor the heritage of Hanslick. I saw Beckmesser in various models both plump and slender, marking the faults and foul points on the green covers of the Universal Edition. Thus nothing changes. Except that Mahler is no more, and Bruno Walter has risen from his place in the audience to the podium . . . Anyone who did not witness the paleness of Bruno Walter, forced to come back a dozen times and bow to those

frantic with love intermingled among sneerers full of hate, cannot convey the intensity of emotion and the stormy ardor that differentiates a Mahler premiere from any other.[4]

Stormy ardor, both pro and con, is indeed apparent in the earliest accounts of *Das Lied von der Erde*, beginning with that of its first listener, Alma Mahler.

According to Alma, during 1909 and 1910 Mahler "played bits of *Das Lied von der Erde* to me almost daily . . . I knew it by heart before it was first performed." Even though Mahler was denied his usual revisions and retouchings, Alma declares that "I cannot imagine his altering a note in a work so economical in its means of expression."[5] And as noted earlier, it was she who made the striking connection between "Der Abschied" and the boy Mahler's extraordinarily patient, trusting reverie as afternoon merged into twilight when he was left alone in the woods by his father.[6] William Ritter provides us the touching detail that at the premiere, during the second movement at the lines "Ich komm' zu dir, traute Ruhestätte! ja gib mir Ruh' . . . [I come to you, beloved resting place! Yes, give me peace]," Alma could no longer maintain her composure.[7]

Evidently the next person to become acquainted with the work was Bruno Walter, who reports the circumstances thus:

> He turned the manuscript over to me for study; for the first time, it was not from himself that I became familiar with a new work. When I brought it back to him, almost unable to utter a word, he turned to the *Abschied* and said: "What do you think? Is that to be endured at all? Will not people do away with themselves after hearing it?" Then he pointed out the rhythmic difficulties and asked jokingly: "Have you any idea how one is supposed to conduct this? I haven't!"[8]

This meeting took place in Vienna shortly after the premiere of the Eighth Symphony in September 1910. "I studied the work and lived through days of a most violent mental upheaval," Walter writes. "I was profoundly moved by that uniquely passionate, bitter, resigned, and blessing sound of farewell and departure, that last confession of one upon whom rested the finger of death."[9] Walter duly led the first performance of *Das Lied* on 20 November 1911, almost exactly six months after Mahler's death, as part of a two-day memorial celebration in Munich, the city of the Eighth's rousing premiere, under the management of its "Barnum-and-Bailey" impresario, Emil Gutmann. The first concert was a Mahler *Liederabend* given by one of his singers from the Vienna Opera, alto Sarah Charles Cahier, with Walter at the piano. *Das Lied von der Erde* opened the second evening, with tenor William Miller and Mme. Cahier as soloists, and Bruno Walter conducting the Munich Konzertverein Orchestra; to conclude the program, which lasted a full three hours, Walter had chosen the "Resurrection" Symphony, obviously to mitigate the melancholy of the new work, as several critics noted. According to William Ritter, Walter pushed himself beyond all limits in preparing the concerts, just as Mahler himself so often had. There were five and a half hours of full rehearsal each day beginning on Thursday, 16 November; in addition, on Saturday evening Walter coached the soprano soloist for the Second Symphony, then left at eight for Augsburg where he rehearsed the chorus until midnight, and caught the train back to Munich at one in the morning. Sunday, the day of the public dress rehearsal, began with placement of the chorus and rehearsal of the Second's choral conclusion with orchestra. When the doors opened to the audience at 11:45, Sarah Charles Cahier was not present, having missed her train connection in Saarbrücken. Therefore the Symphony had to be performed first at the dress rehearsal, followed by the three tenor songs of *Das Lied*; Madame Cahier arrived at length to sing the three movements for alto solo. That evening, of course, she and Walter gave their *Liederabend*. "This is what Mahler died from," Ritter wryly observes.[10]

Although it is beyond the scope of a small volume such as this to present comprehensive coverage of the early reactions to *Das Lied*, we can sample enough critiques of the Munich premiere to gauge both the general flavor of such reviews and their rather predictable division into camps, depending upon the orientation of the commentator. A noteworthy announcement of the first performance appeared in *Der Merker* (first November issue of 1911), the music periodical founded in 1909 by Richard Batka and Richard Specht, two critics favorably disposed towards Mahler's music; Specht, in fact, had already written the first biography of the composer (1905), and had spoken personally with him on a few occasions.[11] It is unclear who provided the information in the *Merker* notice. The most likely contributors are: Specht himself; Bruno

Walter, who is identified as "editing Mahler's artistic *Nachlaß*"; and Alma Mahler, whose assured presence at the event is prominently announced at the end. But at least part of this material was also included in a press release issued by Gutmann, which is not currently known to survive. Indeed, the whole purpose of the *Merker* announcement was probably to influence the critics' agenda in their reviews. Calling *Das Lied* as much a "formal novelty" as the Eighth Symphony, *Der Merker* claims the designation "Symphony for Large Orchestra . . . with Tenor and Alto Soloists" – which is very nearly what Mahler entitled it – is inadequate: "Most succinctly, the work is to be characterized as a new sort of 'Lied-Symphony.'"[12] Thereby genre and its significance – an issue hotly debated by some critics after the premiere of the Eighth – were brought to the foreground even before *Das Lied* was performed. Another problem highlighted by the article is that of autobiographical influence upon the expressive import of the work. About this the author(s) are also explicit:

> The principal spiritual idea [*geistige Leitidee*] of the entire work is the expression of the utterly consummate turning away from the world and world-denial [*vollkommenste Weltabkehr und Weltverneinung*] that were Mahler's worldview in his last years. The sixth movement is staggering; it is filled with the artist's presentiment of death, and represents a gripping lament and accusation [*Klage*] over his loneliness and his being misunderstood.

A kernel of truth underlies this passage, as we have seen. Yet the claim that Mahler's attitude toward the world was completely negative during his last years is exaggerated: his letters and the record of his professional activities prove otherwise. Neither Walter nor Specht is likely to have made such a blunt assessment on his own authority. But Alma could have done so, and as suggested above, she may have had a reason. Alma knew that her affair with Gropius during the summer of 1910 had shattered Mahler, yet she initially had no intention of giving it up: in September she held secret trysts with Gropius in Munich while Mahler was rehearsing the Eighth, and did so again in October during her trip to Paris (without Mahler) en route to America. She also planned to return to Europe before Mahler in the spring of 1911. (Alma's mother, Anna Moll, helped keep matters secret and facilitated the exchange of the lovers' passionate correspondence.) Alma considered this liaison due compensation for the frustrations, both sexual and artistic, of her marriage to Mahler; only with the onset of his final illness did she suspend her meetings with Gropius (although their correspondence continued).[13] As de La Grange has frequently pointed out, depicting Mahler as a sick, depressed old man in his last years, which Alma tends to do in her published memoirs, was probably an effort to justify the infidelity that caused Mahler such anguish during his final months. The *Merker* notice may represent her first public statement to that effect; indeed, at the time of *Das Lied*'s premiere, rumors were already circulating in the newspapers that Alma would remarry in America.[14] She flirted heavily with the conductor Otto Klemperer at this time, had a brief liaison with the composer Franz Schreker, then began her tempestuous affair with the painter Oskar Kokoschka the following spring.[15] And Alma's view of Mahler's declining spirits is partially contradicted by Klemperer, who saw a good deal of him during preparations for the premiere of the Seventh Symphony in September 1908 – i.e., just after *Das Lied von der Erde* had been drafted:

> It would be a grave mistake to regard Mahler as a world-weary man. The best biography that has been written about him [i. e., in 1948] is by his wife Alma Mahler, who also emphasizes these traits. I myself, since I was privileged to know Mahler, can vouch that he was of a very lively, even cheerful nature. He could become very angry only with those who failed to do their duty ...
>
> The last song in *Das Lied von der Erde* is "Der Abschied." It was his farewell to life, and the piece is profoundly moving. Right at the end can be heard the words: "I go, I wander, I seek peace for my lonely heart." For even if, as I have said, he was by nature lively and by no means world-weary, he was nonetheless a lonely man. He died too early.[16]

A feuilleton that appeared in the Halle *Saale-Zeitung* (25 October 1911) also designates the new form of the work as "Lied-Symphony," but emphasizes that "the motivic transformation of the execution, and above all the extraordinary unity of style not to be found in any of Mahler's earlier works, justifies the designation of symphony (with obbligato solo voice)." (The author notes that Wöss's piano reduction was already circulating in proofs, and it seems likely that he had obtained it, or was in close touch with someone in Vienna.) Here again, turning from the world (*Weltabkehr*) is identified as the principal idea

(*Leitidee*) of the work, in which Mahler, "this genius of the path of metaphysical development [*metaphysischer Entwicklungsweg*] comes to an end in pessimism and finally finds in the negation of the world [*Welt-verneinung*] the adequate expression of his worldview . . . The new work reveals the profile, turned away from the world, of one resigned . . . Henceforth the soul of the artist vibrates and feels in the abandoned spheres of his loneliness, and finds there only the vast expression of lament." The author then provides a brief but insightful characteriza-tion of each movement: "Das Trinklied vom Jammer der Erde" is "a weighty but spirited [*schwungvolles*] Allegro for the tenor that sets forth as an introduction the motto of refusing the world: 'Dunkel ist das Leben, ist der Tod [Dark is life, dark is death].'" The second song, "Der Einsame im Herbst," is "an infinitely sweet *espressivo* of the presenti-ment of death," while the following two movements "reflect upon the nullity of earthly life, the emptiness of striving and material beauty, with more cheerful resignation." "Von der Jugend" is described as "a little Chinese rococo picture" that "ingeniously ironizes the instability of materiality, in that the picture is also simultaneously turned on its head (in the reflection of the water)." The author views "Von der Schönheit" as a kind of trio to the preceding scherzo that has become independent of it and "celebrates the sweet eros of the world." "The fifth movement, 'Der Trunkene im Frühling' . . . reiterates once again the spiritual lacer-ation [*Zerrissenheit*] of one gone awry of the world. The musical emo-tional content of the movement is a 'hopeless case' ['*Desperando*'] of startling wondrousness . . ." "Der Abschied," however, which out-wardly comprises a third (*sic*) of the entire work, is "more than a finale. In this gripping epilogue to his own life, the artist speaks for himself alone. Lonely he stands in the fading world, and, as once again from the intoxication of nature the ancient voice of earthly life resounds in him, he waits for Death . . . In a long-drawn-out *morendo*, soul and longing waft away into eternity." Drawing attention to the unusual final chord of C major with added A, and to the "heavenly voice of the celesta," the article concludes: "The song of earth dies away [*erstirbt*], life has ceased to suffer."

Among those in attendance at the premiere were the young composers Anton Webern and Alban Berg, both devoted disciples of Arnold Schoenberg's. Their master, however, was unable to make the journey to

Munich because he was preoccupied with a lecture series in Berlin, where he and Webern had recently relocated. Although Schoenberg was not initially an unreserved Mahler enthusiast, a performance of the Third Symphony in 1904 had completely won him over; in his famous Prague memorial lecture of 1912 he would declare that "Gustav Mahler was a saint."[17] And while Mahler was uncertain about the value of Schoenberg's music, he nevertheless supported his gifted young colleague, even to the point of silencing hecklers at scandalous Schoenberg premieres and anonymously purchasing some of his paintings. Schoenberg and his students were among the coterie who would travel long distances to hear Mahler's music, and all of them regarded him as an important musical ancestor. Mahler met with them on more than one occasion, and they were among the crowd gathered at the Westbahnhof in December 1907 to say farewell as the Mahlers departed Vienna for their first season in America.[18]

Webern arrived in Munich in time to attend some of the rehearsals of *Das Lied*, and wrote to Schoenberg on 18 November:

> I have just heard Mahler's "Lied von der Erde." I cannot speak. Standing next to Frau Mahler, I was allowed to read along with her in Mahler's *handwritten* score. I cannot tell you how happy that made me: The wife of the immortalized one encouraged me to read along with her in the score written by Mahler himself. Only she and I read it. Sometimes I had it to myself. I have behind me hours that I count among the things that were and are dearest to me.
>
> I had the feeling that Mahler had so ordained it that I, since I was to hear the "Lied von der Erde" for the first time, had in hand the score written by himself. Yes, Herr Schoenberg, if only you had been there. This music – there is nothing I can say.
>
> Be well, my dear Herr Schoenberg, I cannot write any more, my God, I would like more than anything else to give up the ghost.
>
> Yours, Webern[19]

Back in Berlin, on 22 November Webern played *Das Lied* on the piano for Schoenberg, whose diary records that "We could not speak." The next day he wrote two letters to close friends and fellow composers in Vienna. To Paul Königer he observed that "Das Lied von der Erde is the most marvellous creation that exists. When one is dying, images of one's life are said to pass before one's soul – so it is with this work. It cannot be

described in words. What power exerts itself here!"[20] And in a letter to
Berg his enthusiasm seems boundless:

> Yesterday I was together with Schoenberg almost the whole day. In the
> forenoon I played him the "Lied von der Erde" – what a title! He was
> deeply affected. We could not speak. What you wrote [me] about the Lied
> von der Erde is wonderful. As I put it to you before, it is like the passing of
> life, or better, of what was lived in the soul of the dying person. The work
> of art condenses, dematerializes; the factual dissolves, the idea remains;
> that's how these songs are. I want to say more to you about details. How
> remarkable is the glockenspiel in the first movement. This gleam, the way
> it comes in this fundamentally despairing movement. And in the second
> [movement] the passage: "Ich komm zu Dir, treue Ruhestätte, ja, gib mir
> Ruh' [I come to you, faithful resting place, yes, give me rest]" (the D here
> in the bass clarinet alone, do you remember that note) – "ich hab Erquick-
> ung Not [I need refreshment]," that is the pinnacle of music, or earlier the
> place with the solo cello (only what's the text, I have to look it up) oh yes:
> "Bald werden die verwelkten goldenen Blätter der Lotusblumen auf dem
> Wasser ziehen.[Soon the withered golden leaves of the lotus blossoms will
> float upon the water]" – I could play this music forever. Yes, now tell me,
> do you know what it is that is so telling here and in the utterances of other
> great men; have you ever pondered that; what happens when you hear
> such a thing? What is this unutterable quality? I have something that
> orients me, although of course nothing is explained thereby – I believe in
> God. – – – The third song is called "Von der Jugend." The title comes
> from Mahler. I told Königer I took it to mean that youth sees things
> turned the wrong way, in "mirror image [Spiegelbild]." That's not so
> important to me now, perhaps the interpretation is superfluous, or maybe
> wrong. Königer thought the point is this lovely, carefree image, and so it
> is. "Freunde, schön gekleidet, trinken, plaudern [friends, beautifully clad,
> drinking, chatting]", and yet the "reflection [Spiegelung]"??! My dear, in
> IV "Zwischen Büschen und Blättern sitzen sie, sammeln Blüten [Amidst
> bushes and leaves they sit, gathering blossoms]" etc. There music conveys
> absolutely the highest expression of loveliness; what an image: the girls in
> between blossoms and the sunshine. You have surely felt something
> similar and struggled with how to express it. Isn't this passage beyond
> words, here again resounds this sweetness, this loveliness. And the par-
> allel spot "In dem Dunkel ihrer großen Augen [In the darkness of her
> large eyes] etc." – Schoenberg once said to me that there is in addition, or

perhaps on the whole, a very different sort of love other than the passion sanctioned by literature, namely this quiet, above all sweet, charming connection. This is the only way I have felt it, not otherwise, which is to say differently after all, you know, sadly, ah Berg, it is probably beyond words. But here is the very same thing; here in Mahler, just think of this sweetness in the music: "In dem Dunkel ihres heißen Blicks schwingt klagend noch die Erinnerung ihres Herzens nach [In the darkness of her hot glance the recollection of her heart still reverberates plaintively within her]." – It is to pass away, to die. – And even so the "Trunkene im Frühling" . . . "Weil Kehl' und *Seele* voll [Because throat and *soul*[21] are full]." "Taumelnd [reeling]," to be drunk, drunk in the soul, if that cannot be, to die, in animal agitation[.] "Ich frag ihn, ob schon Frühling sei, mir ist als wie im Traum [I ask him whether it's already spring, it's as though I am in a dream]." The solo violin, "the piccolo"! And the contrabassoon in the passage "Aus tiefstem Schauen lausch' ich auf [In deepest gazing I 'listened up']," that's really the most enigmatic thing ever. Back during the rehearsal when I heard that for the first time, I would best have liked to give up the ghost. Can you still hear the harps at the spot in the VIth song "Ich spüre eines feinen Windes Hauch [I sense the breath of a delicate breeze]" and then the low C of the basses, the long pause! – Ah, dear Berg, I can say no more about these things. "O Schönheit, o ewigen Liebens, lebens-trunkne Welt [O beauty, O world drunk of eternal love-and-life]," "Du, mein Freund [You, my friend]" . . . Often I think, well, is one permitted to hear this – do we deserve that? But we must strive after it such that we do deserve it. To reach deeply into the heart, cast off the muck, upwards, "sursum corda [lift up your hearts]" as the Christian religion says. Thus Mahler lived, thus Schoenberg. There is repentance and there is longing.

> Yours, Webern

Among the first printed reviews to appear was that by Rudolf Louis in the *Münchner Neueste Nachrichten* (22 November 1911), the most important paper in the Bavarian capital. Louis, who also achieved recognition as a music theorist, was openly antisemitic and opposed to Mahler; echoing Wagner's denouncement of Jewishness in music, Louis had already claimed that Mahler "speaks musical German . . . with the accent, the cadence, and above all the gesture of the excessively oriental Jew."[22] Criticizing Mahler's "striving after popular national simplicity and smoothness" as both symphonist and lied composer, he dismisses the sixteen songs performed the first night of the festival thus: "Indeed, the more he approaches the manner of the folk song in certain external aspects of his musical speech, all the more strongly one feels the painfully ungenuine [*peinlich Unechte*] that is the real hallmark of Mahlerian music even in this expressive realm [i.e., the lied]." As he had objected to Mahler's calling the Eighth a symphony, so, too, Louis denies that title to *Das Lied*, suggesting it should more properly be called a "Suite" because it is nothing other than a row of six orchestral songs "that one could probably say belong together, but which in no way create the overall impression of a whole that is uniformly closed and organized within itself as do the four movements of a well-constructed symphony." Praising Bethge's poems, Louis acknowledges that they might prove attractive to a composer, yet notes that it requires a great deal of self-confidence to venture "such an immeasurably difficult task, quite apart from the question whether it is not sinful in any case to set to music poems that are so complete as such," thereby perhaps detracting from their poetic beauties.

Louis sees no new side of Mahler in *Das Lied von der Erde*: "In this work, too, I have the impression of a very high-striving artistic will lacking real creative *ability*." To be sure, it contains less of what is most immediately repulsive in most of the other symphonies, and that it does not, on the whole, seek powerful outward effect strikes Louis favorably. But he finds that "sensitive listeners are most disagreeably moved" when a composer "takes the speech of our genuine German masters into his mouth and comports himself as though he were one of them." "Der Einsame im Herbst" made the "strongest, or rather most serious impression" on him; the middle numbers (3 and 4) are "lovingly painted and, particularly as regards sonority, in part very charming display pieces [*Kabinettstücke*]." But he finds the composer lagging farthest behind the poet in the first and fifth songs, where "the expression of 'drunkenness' certainly lacks everything that would convincingly sweep one away with it." The first part of "Der Abschied" is "so monotonous that the sweet, somewhat too sweet conclusion tends no longer to be properly effective." In sum, Louis considers the work by far less effective than the "Resurrection" Symphony with which it was coupled, and which seems very much the opposite of *Das Lied*. Without saying anything new about the

Second, he finds it necessary to repeat that as regards "mass effect [*Massenwirkung*] (the effect *through* and *upon* the masses) Mahler did not subsequently equal this symphony (not even in the Eighth)." In addition, Louis was alone among the critics in his reserved attitude toward Bruno Walter's conducting; the rest were unstinting in their praise. Later in the same day that his review was published in Munich, an unsigned synopsis of it appeared in the *Wiener Abendpost*, where the principal critic was Robert Hirschfeld, Mahler's most outspoken enemy in Vienna.

Rudolf Louis reiterated his objections, embellished with additional polemical barbs, in a second review of *Das Lied von der Erde* that appeared in the *Rheinische Musik- und Theater-Zeitung* (2 December 1911). To his credit, he suggests in a footnote that Bethge's *Nachdichtungen* may not be true to the original Chinese poetry – a problem that has occupied scholars until very recently. But even more than in his Munich review, Louis here stresses that Mahler's creative powers were not equal to Bethge's (a position no one would defend today). Again claiming that Mahler's "high-flying artistic will, which ventures toward the most sublime things with a childlike, naive self-confidence and a more distinguished knowledge of orchestral than of compositional technique" is not matched by creative ability worthy of the name, Louis declares that "in this work as well, Mahler's music is essentially impotent." In his view Mahler's eclectic borrowings have only increased over time, and now include debts to Strauss, the "new French," and "new Italians" as well. In this review Louis is explicit about "what often immediately repulses and disgusts one in Mahler," namely "the trivial and banal, the unctuously mawkish, and the offensively sentimental [*das schmierig Süßliche und widerlich Sentimentale*]," which, he concedes, is "far rarer" in *Das Lied* than elsewhere. In so far as it was possible for him to do so, Mahler has here avoided outward effect, yielding "a general impression, which one very seldom gets in Mahler, of artistic propriety."

Enthusiasts were not slow to praise Mahler's posthumous work. Among them was the world-famous dermatologist Arthur Neisser of Breslau (a cousin of Mahler's friend Arnold Berliner's) who dabbled in music journalism. Neisser had been won over by a performance of Mahler's Third in 1904, when he got to know Mahler personally, and he attended rehearsals and the premieres of both the Seventh and Eighth Symphonies.[23] In the Berlin paper *B. Z. am Mittag* (22 November 1911, no. 274), Neisser recalls his anxious forebodings while witnessing Mahler's self-sacrifice during the countless rehearsals for the Eighth: "it was as though the wings of Death already soared over these days of thundering artist's triumph . . . Early presentiments of death must have filled Mahler's soul, ultimately worn away both spiritually and physically, such that he struggled from the heart to bring forth this symphony about the sorrow and transitoriness of all that is earthly, and about the eternity of all beauty in nature. The tune that Mahler sounds here is peculiarly like a monologue." Neisser accepts that the work is a type of "Liedsinfonie," but suggests it is "more a suite of songs bound together only through guiding musical and poetic threads . . . Gustav Mahler sings this gripping swan song [*Schwanengesang*] only with restrained voice, not boiling over as formerly in his symphonies, and he whispers his passion quickly aloft, not, as previously, reveling innocently in folkish tunes in true musicianly manner." Nevertheless, Neisser finds many genuine Mahlerian touches, as, for example, in the "diabolical-sounding drinking music with which the work begins." The most elevated portion of *Das Lied* is the concluding hymn, "when, amidst menacing strokes of the gong, the gates to the realm of the dead open and a dialogue unfolds between the dying one and Friend Death [*dem Freunde Tod*], with tragic power."

Several days later a longer review by Neisser appeared in the *Hamburger Fremdenblatt* (25 November 1911). Here he further underscores the autobiographical dimension in *Das Lied*, suggesting that it may be Mahler's testament to the musical world of how far beyond exaggerated self-worth and self-delusion he really was, despite the fact that as supreme commander of the Vienna Court Opera he occasionally had to take the lead in despotic manner purely for the sake of his beloved art. Neisser praises the literary and graphic [*malerischen*] instincts that animated Mahler throughout his life, as a result of which he knew how to join together six poems whose basic shape would correspond to the Lied-symphony he envisioned. The basic theme of the poems, according to Neisser, "is a sort of Dionysian death-drunkenness [*Todestrunkenheit*]" that "before departure from life, from love, and from reveling in beauty, seeks to be intoxicated one last time by these primeval earthly, and therefore eternal, things." Mahler sought to achieve the contrast of mood that the musical setting of such texts requires through the use of

the alto and tenor soloists. While the tenor is heard in the wanton drinking songs of sorrow, which are irreverent of nature [*naturfrevlerischen*],
and indeed mostly in the intentionally shrillest and highest register, the
"velvet-soft alto" denotes "the appeasing resignation and at the same
time the calm, contemplative philosophy that takes delight in the natural
sounds of the birds and in the moon floating off like a silver sickle on the
heavenly sea . . ." Then, "with a painful smile the dying one reflects one
last time upon the blissful love and beauty of youth, and withdraws resolutely into the evening, and, in the face of Nature falling peacefully
asleep yet ever reawakening, he takes leave forever of the world that is
eternally drunk from love and life."[24]

We should not, in Neisser's view, dispute too much with Mahler
whether in this posthumous work, as so often previously, he has not fully
achieved what he longed for so intensely; rather should we bow before a
great artist's resignation to death and be satisfied with the calm, melancholy joy this "hymn to earth and life" has awakened in our hearts. As
regards the form of a symphony – and here Neisser is probably responding to other critics, such as Louis – he believes the work can be divided
with respect to its expressive shape into Allegro, Adagio, three scherzos,
and a grand finale; symphonic, too, are the leitmotivic developments of
thematic material. But now he takes issue with the notion of a *Liedsym-
phonie*, because "in this work something entirely different has a new and
shocking effect, namely the instrumental use of the solo singing voice in
interweaving with solo instruments." This invention marks Mahler as a
musical landscape painter of the very first rank, which is at least as
important for the public and for future generations as if he had discovered "seven times seven and seventy new harmonies" and had deployed
"seventy-part counterpoint."

As regards multiplicity of instrumental combinations, Mahler has
clearly striven to restrain himself so as not to interfere with the basic
mood of this "song" of the earth. And (perhaps in response to Louis's
characterization of *Kabinettstücke*), Neisser argues that the three scher-
zolike movements (nos. 3–5) contain so many harmonic refinements and
such rhythmic esprit "that the inventive strength of him who was so
readily undervalued in that respect is clearly brought to expression." Of
"Der Abschied" he notes that it is "especially rich in soulful, silver beauty
. . . in the passage where the longing for death achieves breakthrough [*die*

Todessehnsucht zum Durchbruch kommt] with the words 'Ich sehne mich, o Freund, an deiner Seite die Schönheit dieses Abends zu genießen [I long, o Friend, to enjoy the beauty of this evening by your side],' Mahler must have been overcome as though he had really just found the very last friend in his life, which was so filled with abandonments [*in seinem entsagungsreichen Leben*], and a cantilena sounds forth that, in the purity of its line, releases warm tears from us . . . The oppressive conclusion of this song of earthly transitoriness cries out for redemption": therefore Neisser concludes the review of *Das Lied* with praise for Walter's decision to end the concert with the Second Symphony.

An unsigned notice in the *Frankfurter Zeitung* (23 November 1911, 1st morning edn.) wastes few words before declaring that the six movements of *Das Lied* stand together neither in a motivic nor any other musical connection, but rather are held together by the poetic idea of the transitoriness of human life in its heights and depths, joys and sorrows. Monotony, however, is avoided in that the basic musical mood does not correspond to this idea in all parts of the work. The reviewer regards the first movement as probably the most significant of the whole, and characterizes the second as an elegy with awe-inspiring capacity of transition from objective nature-painting to subjective nature-feeling. The third movement is a graceful scherzo in "Chinese rococo" style; "Von der Schönheit" is mentioned only as an Andante with an agitated middle section, and "Der Trunkene im Frühling" as somewhat forced in its humor. "Der Abschied" constitutes "a glance outward into eternity, with the usual musical question mark," apparently referring to the added-sixth chord of the final bars, which had also been noted by Louis.

The critic objects that "the voices are treated with a lack of consideration scarcely to be surpassed," which taxes even such artists as Cahier and Miller. The orchestration he finds grateful in that it encompasses all phases of utterance from the most luxuriant realm of color to aesthetic poverty, yet remains only in an accompanimental role, elucidating and illustrating the songs. As regards the question of genre, the writer views *Das Lied* less as a new "Lied-Sinfonie" than as a number of lieder with orchestral accompaniment put together according to an extramusical viewpoint. And he questions whether "this orchestral accompaniment might be an all-too-pompous raiment," whether smaller or even the smallest forces – i.e., the piano – might have been sufficient. The Second

Symphony, according to this critic, surpasses Mahler's later works in approaching the symphonic ideal, "which is to elevate the individual instance of personal feeling to the significance of a generally valid experience," and this despite the "well-known peculiarities of the Mahlerian score, not to mention in this case [i.e., the Second] the strong influence of Wagner and Bruckner as well."

Ferdinand Keyfel, critic of the *München-Augsburger Abendzeitung*, contributed a favorable review to the periodical *Signale für die musikalische Welt* (vol. 69, no. 48, 29 November 1911).[25] "Mahler had the obstinate courage," he begins, "to dictate new laws to the musical fantasy; such is also the case in the Lied von der Erde." Yet as regards the genre of the composition, Keyfel finds that, notwithstanding unifying motivic and affective factors as well as Mahler's bold innovation in breaking the bonds of symphonic form to create a Lied-symphony, "the song alone determines the invention of the six movements . . . the orchestral edifice grows out of the vocal part." The work is convincing because "Mahler himself lived this song on the earth." Accordingly, Keyfel suggests the best approach to *Das Lied* is to begin with "Der Abschied," which sounds as though it were a premonition of Mahler's own fate. This is truly music of severe loneliness that sings like the mists and waters of a craggy mountain landscape at evenfall. Rather curiously, however, for Keyfel the most original movement is "Von der Jugend," which so successfully imitates "the mood of white Chinese porcelain" in its sound color. His chief criticism of *Das Lied* as a whole is that it lacks decisive moments of repose, so rich is the thematic invention and the continuous motion of harmony and orchestral beauty. "Nevertheless, forgoing all outward effect, Mahler has set forth a frequently staggering beauty, the highest measure of musical feeling in this newest work, the spirit of which can only be accounted for through the eternal supermundane longing of love [*Liebessehnsucht*]."

We have already encountered the writings of William Ritter, the Swiss writer, painter, and art critic living in Munich who had been outraged by his first encounter with Mahler's music (the Fourth Symphony in 1901), but subsequently became a friend and supporter of Mahler's, and was among the coterie in attendance at the premieres of the Seventh and Eighth Symphonies.[26] Ritter issued two lengthy French articles about *Das Lied*, the first of which appeared in the *Gazette de Lausanne* (no. 326, 26 November 1911). Heavily laced with reminiscences, this piece is more a homage to the occasion of the premiere than a review *per se*. Ritter describes his first meeting with Mahler in 1906, at the first rehearsal for the Munich premiere of the Sixth: the composer struck him as "not only a genius, but a rare and divine man, marked by a sort of seal of predestination for suffering and for triumph in death. From the day I first made personal acquaintance with him, I feared for his life. Just the incredible energy that he dispensed was bound to devour such a fragile machine in such poor condition." Ritter would appear to be one of the more reliable witnesses regarding Mahler's legendary fear of naming a Ninth Symphony: at the premiere of the Seventh (Prague, September 1908) Alma told him in confidence that a ninth symphony with Chinese texts was largely finished, but because of his horror of the number nine, Mahler would furtively slip this most recent work under a title until such time as the next symphony was sketched; thereupon it would suddenly bear the number ten, and nine would thus be passed over. Ritter suggests that the triumph of the Eighth probably made Mahler sufficiently confident of the future that he no longer attempted to snare destiny.

Ritter was deeply moved by the first rehearsal of *Das Lied*, at which he was one of only six listeners permitted in the hall:

> What was Mahler thinking of? I wonder whether, having hoped while living to break the "enchantment" of this fateful number nine once and for all, he did not on the contrary prefer, by dying, to become again subject to the inexorable law that presided over the destiny of Beethoven and Bruckner, the two masters from whom he draws so much and whom he held in such veneration? It goes without saying that I advance this proposition as an entirely personal one. None of us dared to ask Madame Mahler anything that she judged it unnecessary to confide in us . . .

Ritter finds *Das Lied* to be "the quintessence of Mahler":

> His *Ninth Symphony*, his *Ode to Joy*, if one would maintain that there was one, his grandiose and formidable conception was his Number VIII. In his apparent preoccupation with eluding the redoubtable associations which this number IX evokes, which also terrified the aging Bruckner, he resolved to take refuge in foreign sides of his nature and to create a work of precious finesse and elegant svelteness.

Postponing more detailed discussion for a future occasion, he offers a striking summary of the new work's character:

> The spirit of old Vienna, so nostalgic, which is found in the *altväterisch* ["grandfatherly"] scherzo [i.e., trio] of the Sixth Symphony and the night music movements of the Seventh, allies itself with a certain exotic vagueness of intent [*velléité exotique*], which does not conspicuously seek to "sinologize," but which Mahler had naturally in his disposition. Put another way, under the pretext of *chinoiserie* he has given fair play to everything particularly odd and whimsical [*bizarre*] that was mixed into the profound and generous humanity of his vehement and tender nature. Even in Prague [at the Seventh's premiere] he said to us: "Oh! Chinese? That would be the most Mahlerian thing of all! [*Ce sera avant tout du Mahler!*]"

Ritter's second article (*La Vie Musicale* 5/7 [1 December 1911]: 136–40) is perhaps the most perceptive review of the premiere. Following introductory remarks cited in part above (pp. 55–56), he addresses the much-debated question of genre by insisting that the work is "purely symphonic," consisting of a sonata-form first movement and a proper finale, as well as an Andante and diverse scherzos or intermezzos. These are not songs accompanied by orchestra; rather, it is the orchestra that takes on voice here. Ritter offers the prescient suggestion that Mahler tends to blend song and symphony throughout his oeuvre, even as he also seeks to reconcile the symphony and the symphonic poem: "the subject of the symphonic poem in all the works of Mahler is the states of soul of his own life, a life of love, of intelligence, of work and of sorrow, and under the sway of sublime summonses to the consolation of human distress, to nostalgic evocation of past happiness, to the invocation of a better world, to justice, and to the peace of God." The suffering in Mahler's work "is among the most poignant that exists in music" because it does not overwhelm itself and disappear; rather, Mahler sang it with the courage to leave it behind as he pursues his upward path: "he sets forth, he continually parts company." For Ritter, texts such as "I am of God, and will return to God" (from "Urlicht" in the Second Symphony) are always present – even if not literally, the musical sense of them is there. Therein lies the Jewish component in Mahler, if one would insist on finding it: "He knows he is among the elect; he goes straight ahead on his path." Thus, all who have suffered and wept with and through Mahler were never the essence, the true foundation of his art, but rather "*a means of messianic proclamation [un moyen de messiation]*." This special dimension, even while thoroughly imbued with the sacred sediment of humanity, is nevertheless above flesh, blood, and tears. "It is also through this that his music addresses itself *to everyone, to the elite of souls,*" and not at all to the self-designated elite of the intelligentsia, the mandarins, and the philistines.

As evidence of this "quality of soul" in Mahler, Ritter draws attention to his alterations in the Bethge texts, and particularly to those lines interpolated at the close of "Der Abschied," beginning with "Ich wandle nach der Heimat, meiner Stätte [I am travelling to the homeland, to my abode]" (cf. the translation in the Appendix, p. 131 below). Mahler's choice of Chinese texts was not merely a pretext for exotic effects; rather, "he recognized here the same voice of the Orient that spoke of paradise lost in his blood." The underlying unity of the work is the same tendency found in Mahler overall, "to represent a human life in its totality, to make human life a symphony." Ritter then draws an extraordinary parallel between the grand diptych of the Eighth Symphony and the outer movements of *Das Lied von der Erde*. In the Eighth, the welcome of the divine mother opening the gates to heaven (part II) is extended to "Faust-Adam, who just now [part I] was crying in the thousand voices of his commonplace heart: *Veni creator spiritus* [Come, creator spirit]. . . ." Both the first and last movements of *Das Lied* contain "the appeal to Death as liberator": in the first movement, it is "a call ironic and terrible, philosophical and swaggering"; in the finale, "resigned and tender, confident, imploring, and gentle. That is the basis of the work, which henceforth decomposes itself accordingly [*dès lors se décompose ainsi*]."

After brief yet colorful characterizations of the individual movements, Ritter notes that although the large Mahlerian orchestra is present, its treatment is leaner, airier, more flexible, and more refined under pretext of retreat into the past, the vague Chinese tint, and the exotic atmosphere – "Mahler without puffiness or overtaxing. Mahler washed on satin by the brush of a Japanese watercolorist. . . . And at long intervals a return, discreet and fleeting, of the savage Mahler of vast cataclysms of despair . . ." Ritter draws particular attention to what he regards as a striking alpine quality ("l'impression *alpestre*") in "Der Abschied," and suggests that for a long time to come the "most beautiful alpine 'states of soul'" will be found in the works of Mahler. "And I repeat, as I have repeated my [claim of] messianism, that the secret of such melodic freshness has been lost since Schubert, and that of such warmth of heart since Smetana."

The day after the premiere Vienna's most influential newspaper, the *Neue freie Presse*, carried a brief and positive report characterizing *Das Lied von der Erde* as the "grippingly affective voluntary confession of the composer who had become resigned and withdrawn from the world, and who here takes farewell from youth, beauty, and external life, in moving songs of uncommon concentration and most sorrowful melody." Two weeks after the event (4 December) the same paper carried a substantial feuilleton by Richard Specht. The "feuilleton" was a literary or cultural essay concentrating on colorful expression of the author's personal response to an experience, and it was regarded by many Viennese as the epitome of journalism. To have an essay accepted by the *NfP* meant that a writer had "arrived"[27] – and in this case, that Specht, once second-string critic for a less prestigious paper, was being duly recognized as a Mahler specialist. He likens these orchestral songs to the *Four Serious Songs* (*Vier ernste Gesänge*) Brahms wrote near the end of his life, and suggests that *Das Lied* is perhaps Mahler's best work, certainly his most personal. But he finds the mood of farewell much more removed, resigned, and transfigured than in the Brahms songs: "an almost unbearably quiet sorrowfulness speaks here in lofty, relinquishing mildness, very softly, entirely without pathos and without grand gestures; the peaceful voice of one who knows . . ." Specht finds that *Das Lied* manifests the aura of the "last" work because Mahler, frightened by premonitions following the death of his daughter, "really believed that he would then lay down his pen and that no other work would follow this one." (This information is not found in any other source, but it is possible Specht heard it from Mahler, or perhaps from Alma.) Indeed, Specht regards *Das Lied* as "a self-portrait from Mahler's last period. The Song of the Earth has become the 'Lied von Gustav Mahler.'"

Specht suggests that for Mahler the appeal of the oriental poetry, "the sublimated sediment of a very ancient and illustrious culture," lay in the touchingly innocent humanity and universality beneath its splendor; what *Wunderhorn* poetry was for the young man, the "seemingly foreign world of these Chinese songs, iridescent with all sorts of primitive jewels" becomes for the master. The basic themes of both collections are the same: "love and work, need and longing, war and wine, and behind all of that, vast Nature, ever the same, unmoved and uncompassionate." In the first movement, which begins "orgiastically, glowing hot, in drunkenness of depression," Specht identifies both the recurring song-like refrain and the complete symphonic form, which has been "almost epigrammatically condensed." Yet such may not be apparent at first hearing because the whole flows forth with such sovereign freedom as well as melodic impetus arching from beginning to end.

In *Das Lied von der Erde* there is nothing of the purported "extravagance of architecture," "glaring contrasts," and "trivialities" that were style-building principles in the first seven symphonies; therefore, Specht insists that the usual objections of Mahler foes must be withdrawn in this case. Nor is there any of the Mahlerian woodcut-humor that, in its folksy effusions and march rhythms, was formerly used to provide the contrast of a scurrilous little world against the pathos of high tragedy. The melodic style here is unique, so compellingly ripe and accomplished that this manner of speech cannot be mistaken for any other. Whereas in earlier works Mahler's grotesque, Hoffmannesque humor sought to overcome the "burlesque of being" as a palliative for sorrow, "in the late works this humor has turned into a superior sort, more conscious and more vanquishing of pain, and particularly in the 'Song of the Earth,' of a completely transcendental self-possession and gracefulness and contemplativeness blessed by love." Such is most apparent in the third, fourth, and fifth movements.

Specht's descriptions of the inner movements are equally florid. Most telling are his summation of "Der Einsame im Herbst" as "an autumn landscape in tones," and his simile for "Von der Schönheit" – "as though Klinger's *Phantasien* had become music," a reference to the artist whose work was much admired by the Viennese secessionists. In the middle section with the boys on horseback, Mahlerian polyphony has reached its consummation: "nowhere is there greater harshness, nowhere more rough collision, yet overall the sound and clarity of a singing and reveling of many voices, which ally themselves to a single huge song."

Like many listeners, Specht was most moved by "Der Abschied": "few pieces speak such a similarly shocking language." As had Ritter, he draws attention to the "heart-rending, heavily confessional words and verses" Mahler added to the texts, which express the composer's inner world. One such case occurs in "Der Trunkene im Frühling" with the line "Aus tiefstem Schauen lauscht' ich auf [in deepest gazing I 'listened up']," "which practically sums up his being." Another is "Still ist mein Herz und harret seiner Stunde [Still is my heart, and awaits its hour]," which

> discloses his state of mind, completely isolated and no longer hoping for anything – this tonelessly whispered word after the sigh "mir war auf dieser Welt das Glück nicht hold [in this world Fortune was not favorable to me]" has in its unpathetic simplicity an effect that no one can escape, and has in the music, in the evaporating transparency of these sounds of most intensive sweetness and sorrowfulness, which are entirely incorporeal and wholly transformed to spirit, a power to which even those must succumb who lack human interest in this overpowering *confiteor*, and who feel here only the eternal tragedy of the artist fashioned with unspeakable purity.

For Specht nothing in this finale is based on outward effect; everything is inwardly oriented. He regards it as the farewell greeting, moving to the point of tears, of a great man who in reality soon had to depart. Never was Mahler more personal than in this resonant testimony, drawn through all filters of sorrowful humanity, of unearthly purity.

For *Der Merker* (first December issue, 1911) Specht wrote a less stylized essay, which he later incorporated into his well-known *Gustav Mahler* of 1913, the book Schoenberg praised as preserving Mahler's spirit within it.[28] This review includes two noteworthy anecdotes. First, Mahler once dared to hope (without intending any direct comparison between himself and Mozart) that if Mozart could be called "the singer of love," perhaps he could be called "the singer of nature." And second, after completing *Das Lied von der Erde*, he would often sink to his knees in a fragrant field or kiss the petals of a rosebud, so powerful were his feelings about the unity of all being and the eternal love of becoming, versus the necessity of taking leave of life.

Specht considers the first movement "perhaps the most forceful, compact, and peculiar thing Mahler has said in tones: there is a splendor, a brightness about it, an insolence of doubt, a foaming-up of bitterness, irony, ecstasy, and drunkenness, yet simultaneously a conscious sinking into the eternal riddle of life . . ." Obviously in disagreement with criticism such as that of Louis, Specht here and elsewhere insists that the music is chiefly responsible for the work's overall spiritual and artistic unity, to which the poem contributes "only individual conceptual elements as a keynote." He offers here an even better summation of the second movement than he had in the *NfP* feuilleton: "Pedal point of the autumn wind. Rondo of falling leaves." In "Von der Jugend," a charming picture-like piece (as are the following two), "the spectator is already beyond this world, which his glance once again envelops, and which he, with the benevolent smile of the blessed, allows us to observe together with him through his eyes." (This is nearly the same imagery of blessed repose Mahler himself had used to characterize music "lost to the world" in the Adagio of the Fourth Symphony.[29]) "Von der Schönheit" "begins and ends as a most gracious, sweetly erotic minuet";[30] Specht is probably the first to note that the middle portion of the movement is based on motives from its beginning, which he interprets as differentiation of feminine and masculine elements of the same theme: what had been graciously shimmering, full of longing, and caressing becomes equally resolute, light-hearted, and carelessly harsh (cf. Ex. 6, p. 100 below).

"With defiance and indifference 'Der Trunkene im Frühling' preaches the pleasure of intoxication and the shrugging off of toil and trouble." Yet even more than in his earlier review, Specht draws special attention to the passage "aus tiefstem Schauen lauscht' ich auf," where the bird announces the arrival of spring "in one of the sweetest and most moving inspirations of Mahlerian music," which is then shunted aside with defiant gesture: thereby the scurrilous humor is replaced by a tragic vein, "which the music makes comprehensible chiefly through contrasting that mood of reverie and longing with the almost exaggerated boisterousness and unruliness of all the rest." And this, he observes, provides the transition to "Der Abschied."

Again Specht emphasizes the sadness and despair of the finale, in which one now reconciled [*ein Versöhnter*], whom life has brought only deception, quietly departs with minimal display. The melodic quality is incorporeal, unearthly, and has about it something of "'the world-breath's billowing resonance' [*'des Weltatems wehendem Hall'*]": he alludes here to the final lines of Isolde's Transfiguration at the close of *Tristan* – a remarkable insight into the ancestry of "Der Abschied."[31]

Specht also draws attention to Mahler's special use of polyrhythms, which he rightly regards as different from Strauss's or Reger's; so, too, is the style of Mahler's polyphony. And the concluding "ewig" sounds to him as though coming from an unknown star.

In Specht's view, each of Mahler's works is a confession and a piece of autobiography, but none has the equivalent effect of painful beauty and shocking tragedy. While acknowledging that he may be too close to the work to assess its eternal value, he nevertheless asserts that

> for those coming after us as well, "Das Lied von der Erde" will be among Mahler's oeuvre what "The Tempest" is to Shakespeare, the C♯ minor Quartet to Beethoven, "Tristan" to Wagner, and "Tasso" to Goethe: a self-release, a most personal expression of their being. Therein also lies the greatness of this work. And in the alienation from life of its creator, who just for that reason has always been rebuked and misunderstood. But it was ever thus: those of the same mind and same achievement exist only among the mediocre. The greatest was ever the loneliest. Only he who is truly a person unto himself can become a person for everyone.

Far less sympathetic is a review signed "Waghoff" in the Nürnberg-Fürth *Fränkischer Courier* (14 December 1911). The author declares that it is painful always to have to speak of Mahler's incapacity for productive creativity. We continually come up against refined artificiality, brutal mass effects, and, what is worst, lamentable lack of invention. His music is an omnium-gatherum of all possible genres of music, with a particular predilection for trivialities and everyday phrases. The treatment of the voice is often altogether martyrizing, and Mahler is ignorant in that domain to the same degree that he is the greatest connoisseur of orchestral instruments: a mighty expert, but no poet, only a "compose-compiler [*Komponier-Zusammensetzer*]." Waghoff dismisses *Das Lied* as an incomprehensible din and morbid caricatures.

The respected composer, musicologist, and journalist Eugen Schmitz reviewed the premiere of *Das Lied von der Erde* for the *Allgemeine Musik-Zeitung* (vol. 38, no. 48, 1 December 1911, pp. 1230–31).[32] He considers the work no more a symphony than is the Eighth; rather, it is a song cycle for alto, tenor, and large orchestra that contains a lengthy instrumental interlude only in the finale. Schmitz is pleased by Mahler's choice of poetry: "The ever-recurring song of becoming and change, sorrow and joy, coming and going echoes to us here in the remarkably grotesque yet eminently stirring mode of expression of a primeval civilization." Mahler's setting follows the poetic mood with uncommon fineness, from the dallying imagery of sipping tea ("Von der Jugend") and that of brutal ecstasy ("Der Trunkene im Frühling") to silently stammering, suppressed sorrow. The negative side of Mahlerian style, such as the "infamous trivialities" and "percussion orgies of the earlier symphonist," are scarcely in evidence; the orchestration is, on the whole, eminently effective. "All in all, one must count the 'Lied von der Erde' as the *best* that Mahler has yet created: artistically it is above the recently heard Eighth Symphony in the same proportion that it lags behind that work in the squandering of resources."

An unsigned review in the *Strassburger Post* (5 December 1911) also sees *Das Lied* as a group of six songs united both musically and by the theme of earthly sadness. Nevertheless, the work stands very high among Mahler's output: "whoever, like myself, is inwardly a stranger standing in opposition to most of his [Mahler's] compositions, will take a good deal of delight in these *chinoiseries*. To be sure, that fatal blissfulness of sentiment [*fatale Gefühlsseligkeit*] that so often breaks through in his work is not entirely lacking here, and the last movement in particular is so burdened thereby that its many fine features are almost crushed under it." Still, the author finds so much genuine and delicate feeling so artistically formed in this piece that he does not find himself inflamed by the same resistance that overcomes him when listening to most of Mahler's symphonies.

The pianist E.[rika] von Binzer wrote a brief but enthusiastic review for the *Neue Zeitschrift für Musik* (vol. 78, no. 50, 14 December 1911). In her view the new work, which is thrilling in its glowing light and yearning sadness, has borne Mahler to soaring heights in his tonal language, for he achieves the same, or rather kindred and complete triumph only in the Second Symphony, and such seasoned discretion of mood and delicacy of musical apparatus are to be found only in "Urlicht" of the Second, or in passages of the *Kindertotenlieder*. In their sharp characterization these six numbers of his posthumous "symphony" stand in convincingly harmonious relation just as much as, for example, the gravity of the world is tortuous in Mahler's Sixth Symphony. But Binzer regards the work more as a "poem [*Dichtung*]" for solo voices and large orchestra than as a symphony, and like many other critics, considers it "his most intimate confession, the key to the striving and the sorrowful song of this heaven-stormer and stranger to the world," and to be permitted to experience it as such constitutes the greatness and untransitoriness of the event.

4

The music

William Ritter's extraordinary insight into the broad parallel between the "grand diptych" of the Eighth Symphony and the outer movements of *Das Lied von der Erde*[1] takes us to the heart of what Mahler called "the most personal thing I have yet created." Like the oriental doctrine of *Yin* and *Yang* (which Mahler knew from Schopenhauer, and probably other sources), *Das Lied* is founded on syzygial polarities. Yet in this work, as Ritter notes, the opposing forces are ultimately "decomposed." A decisive turning-away from the epic affirmative grandeur of the Eighth, *Das Lied* is ultimately a work of uncertainty: it stops at the moment of liminal transition, and ventures only an inkling of what is beyond. In other respects, as suggested above, the contrast between the two works resembles that between the Third and Fourth Symphonies: massive effects are reduced to more compact forms, textures, and forces, while the "symphonic protagonist" resumes the viewpoint of an isolated individual, represented by two solo singers, on the threshold of life as we know it. The poems Mahler selected and retouched for *Das Lied von der Erde* abound in natural imagery that, in the context of the whole, projects a dualistic conception of the human spirit: night and day, autumn and spring, youth and death, intoxication and meditation, male and female. In basing the work on syzygial pairs, Mahler was not only following his own inner dictates, but also responding to a modernist tendency highly characteristic of *fin-de-siècle* Austrian creative life. As William Johnston has noted, artists and thinkers "as disparate as Freud and Bahr, Mayreder and Weininger, Musil and Kassner, Buber and Broch . . . constructed countless pairs of polar opposites, interweaving the fleeting and the permanent, the present and the past, the manifest and the latent."[2]

On the broadest scale, *Das Lied* is a Mahlerian symphonic structure in two large *Abteilungen*, as shown in Figure 1. Part I comprises the first five

Figure 1   Overall structure of *Das Lied von der Erde*

1	2	3	4	5		6		
Das Trinklied vom Jammer der Erde	Der Einsame im Herbst	Von der Jugend	Von der Schönheit	Der Trunkene im Frühling		Der Abschied		
a	d	B♭	G	A	‖ c	|c	C–a/C	

movements, vignettes of earthly life that last approximately thirty-four minutes in performance. Part II is "Der Abschied," the long moment of departure (approximately twenty-nine minutes): the backdrop for the previous songs, it ultimately absorbs them. The finale is itself a vast binary structure; similarly, the first movement is an almost perfectly symmetrical binary sonata form, as discussed below. The principal tonal centers of the work as a whole are A and C (major or minor: mixture and juxtaposition of mode are stock-in-trade for Mahler). And precisely these two centers are fused into the volatile pentatonic sonority with which "Der Abschied" dissolves on the text "ewig, ewig . . ." (see Ex. 3[b] below). Probably not coincidentally, these are also the principal key areas in the first act of *Tristan und Isolde*, Mahler's favorite work of musical theatre, with which he made his Metropolitan Opera debut on New Year's Day 1908: as we shall see, Isolde's Transfiguration (the so-called "Love-Death" in *Tristan*) almost certainly influenced the final portion of "Der Abschied."

Four of the six movements in *Das Lied* are based on texts explicitly concerned with the problem of death – nos. 1 and 2, and 5 and 6. Paired in their placement, they contrast in style and in vocal range. As Arthur Neisser recognized at the premiere, the dualism of *Das Lied* is immediately apparent in the disposition of the soloists: the tenor is a wanton singer of Dionysian revelry, whereas the alto denotes "appeasing resignation, contemplative philosophy," and Apollonian, autumnal reflection on all that is transitory. This was the voice Mahler had used for the spiritual longing of "Urlicht," which precedes the fresco of Doomsday in the Second Symphony, and also for "O Mensch, gib Acht," the hushed meditation on Nietzschean eternal recurrence in the Third. In *Das Lied* the alto seems to symbolize Mahler's own encapsulation of Goethe's Eternal Feminine:

> that which draws us by mystic force, which every creature, perhaps even the stones, senses with unconditional certainty as the center of its being ... the *resting-place*, the *goal* – as opposed to the eternal longing, striving, and struggling toward this goal – which is the Eternal Masculine.[3]

The two voices, then, do not represent two separate characters (much less the utterances of a narrator), but rather manifest the dynamic polarity of the human spirit.[4] Accordingly, the two soloists present several contrasting views of the end near at hand, all of which were then current in Austrian consciousness. For the tenor in the first song, Death is bitter, a mocking ape howling on the gravestones, interrupting the sweetness of life and the "therapeutic nihilism" of wine. In the fifth, an eternal cycle of drunkenness and sleep are the proper palliatives for care and woe. Dionysian energy commingled with nihilism, irony, and denial is characteristic of these movements. In contrast, the second song, "Der Einsame im Herbst" for alto, epitomizes *Sehnsucht* – a bittersweet alternation of longing for the past and autumnal weariness that breaks into *Todessehnsucht*, the longing for Death as comforter that had long been a facet of the Viennese preoccupation with dying.[5] In "Der Abschied" the same emotions are intensified – "alle Sehnsucht will nun träumen [all longing will henceforth dream]" – culminating in fusion of the protagonist's identity with the figure of Death.

"Das Trinklied vom Jammer der Erde" ("The Drinking Song of Earth's Sorrow")

The opening movement of *Das Lied* is rife with polar tensions. Most obvious is the glaring projection of the singer's drunken bitterness against an extremely tight formal background. Mahler had done something similar on a broader scale in the tragic finale of the Sixth; here all is condensed for more immediate impact. As noted, the movement is almost perfectly symmetrical in its treatment of binary sonata form (see Figure 2). Yet as Robert Bailey has rightly noted, it also embodies characteristics of a strophic lied, most notably in the poignantly despairing

Figure 2   "Das Trinklied vom Jammer der Erde," formal scheme

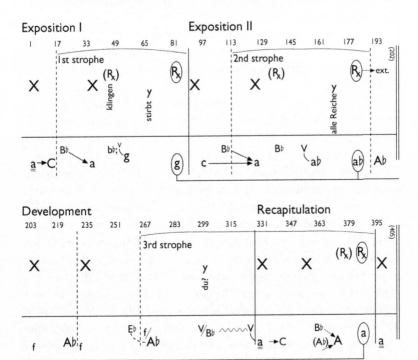

refrain "Dunkel ist das Leben, ist der Tod [Dark is life, dark is death]" heard thrice – at the close of the two "expositions," and finally at the end of the reprise, just before the brief coda ("R" in Ex. 3 below).[6] To achieve this, Mahler compressed Bethge's original four stanzas of text into three, eliminating one occurrence of the refrain. And well along in the compositional process, he hit upon the unusually effective modulatory scheme represented in Figure 2. Initially, the first two stanzas were to be treated strophically, both ending in A (much in the manner of the first song in *Kindertotenlieder*). By the time he wrote out the piano version of this movement, the first stanza concluded with the refrain in A, but the second repeated it in A♭ (as in the published orchestral version); then he corrected the piano score such that the first strophe closes in G minor. The overall result is that the refrain rises by semitone at each recurrence

(G–A♭–A), a deployment of Wagnerian "expressive" tonality that Mahler uses frequently; here it literally heightens the poignant conclusion of each strophe. And each of the expositions modulates, thereby generating the tonal tension essential to sonata form, while neither replicates the other exactly, in accordance with Mahler's long-standing principle that "each repetition is already a lie. A work of art, like life, must always develop itself further."[7]

Although several critics at the premiere of *Das Lied* appreciated its harmonic expressivity, most accorded little significance to the pentatonicism of its musical vocabulary. Even the musicologist Guido Adler, a long-time friend of Mahler's who recognized the cyclical pentatonic "fundamental motive" shown in Ex. 2, considered it "only an incidental attendant phenomenon."[8] But pentatonic scales, the most frequent modes of pitch organization in Eastern music, are central to both horizontal and vertical dimensions of *Das Lied*, and nowhere more so than in the opening movement.[9] They provide Mahler with the germ-motives of the larger structure, which he develops with the same degree of organic coherence that first emerged in the "orientalist" song of 1901, "Ich bin der Welt abhanden gekommen."[10] The first line of Ex. 3 displays the most common pentatonic scales, the anhemitonic or so-called "Chinese," all of which are essentially rotations of the basic form, *Gong*. Ex. 3(b) shows the two triads, A (minor) and C (major), that can be derived from *Gong*, as well as their fusion into the famous "added sixth" sonority that closes *Das Lied*. Two "Japanese" pentatonic forms that do include semitones are shown in Ex. 3(c), which also displays the verticalized subset of scale form *Hirajoshi* that yields a notable dissonant sonority discussed presently. The remainder of Ex. 3 presents the principal motives of the movement, suggesting how the basic cells are woven into them – often with subtle variants, including inversion, augmentation, fragmentation, etc. Harmonic manifestations of the pentatonic motive include the numerous and unusual "V–IV–I" cadential progressions that punctuate this music, most prominently just before the arrival of the refrain (i.e., going into figs. 10, 23, and 45 of the score;[11] scale forms *Shang*, *Zhi*, and *Yu* contain this possible sequence of harmonic roots). Example 4 shows the principal occurrences of the basic cell – a^2–g^2–e^2 in its first appearance – as they coincide with important tonal articulations in the movement. More detailed analysis than can be undertaken here would reveal many additional instances of pentatonic influence. The overall effect of these proce-

Example 2   Cyclic use of the basic pentatonic cell in all movements of *Das Lied von der Erde* (from Guido Adler, *Gustav Mahler* [1916])

(a) 1st mvt., bars 5–9

(b) 2nd mvt., bars 3–6

(c) 3rd mvt., bars 3–6

(d) 4th mvt., bars 8–13

(e) 5th mvt., bars 1–2

(f) 6th mvt., bars 77–80

(g) 6th mvt., bars 167–72

85

Example 3   (a) anhemitonic ("Chinese") pentatonic scales; (b) triads in the anhemitonic pentatonic scale, and triads combined to form the "added sixth" chord; (c) hemitonic ("Japanese") pentatonic scales and derivation of *y* (4–Z29)

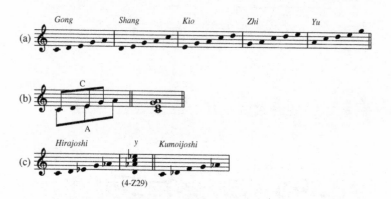

dures is twofold, just as in "Ich bin der Welt": on the one hand, they provide an underlying motivic coherence that is felt well before it is explicitly identified (as is apparent from the earliest reviews of *Das Lied*); on the other, pentatonicism blurs the goal-oriented directionality of traditional functional harmony and counterpoint, yet without displacing their influence entirely. Such pitch coloration combined with delicate orchestration gives the music a decidedly exotic touch.

Three additional factors noted by Theodor Adorno contribute to the exotic quality. One is the "indistinct unison," or heterophony, which crops up earlier in Mahler's Rückert songs and *Kindertotenlieder*, and becomes fundamental to the dissolution that takes place in "Der Abschied."[12] In the opening *Trinklied*, heterophony is already apparent, for example, in the chromaticism of bars 3–4, in the mixed-rhythm arpeggiations between figs. 1 and 2, and the interplay between cellos and tenor four bars before fig. 4 ff.; additional instances are numerous. Another feature is the relative lack of traditional bass function: most of the action is in the upper parts. The functional bass generally moves slowly, and frequently operates not in the lowest register, but in the lower alto or upper tenor ranges (e.g., cellos, violas, horns). A third characteristic is the exceptionally high tessitura of the solo part, which Adorno regards as "a tenor voice extensively denatured in the Chinese manner"; in his view, briefly alluded to above,

Example 3 (*cont.*)   remainder: basic motives and derivations in mvt. 1.

Example 4   Occurrences of the basic pentatonic cell coinciding with significant tonal articulations in mvt. 1.

Das Lied von der Erde has colonized a white area of the intellectual atlas, where a porcelain China and the artificially red cliffs of the Dolomites border on each other under a mineral sky. This Orient is pseudo-morphous also as a cover for Mahler's Jewish element . . . The alienation effects in *Das Lied von der Erde* are faithfully imitated from the irritation that Far Eastern music unalterably causes the Western ear . . . by the euphemism of foreignness the outsider seeks to appease the shadow of terror.[13]

Whether or not one takes Adorno at face value, many passages in this "Drinking Song of Earth's Sorrow" indeed sound strained and out of control, in stark contrast to the taut symphonic form of the movement. The impulse of the quasi-heroic opening horn fanfare ("X" in Ex. 3) is immediately answered by the shrieking chatter of a chromatic descent, colored by the recently discovered technique of flutter-tonguing on the flutes: only in the third strophe will we realize that this is the howling of the monkey on the gravestones, the symbol of death. Two significant features of the work emerge here. (1) Perhaps the most frequent melodic contour in this *Trinklied* is a rising impulse soon followed by a sliding or collapsing descent, often graphically amplified in the orchestra. This seems clearly to project the energetic yet tipsy emotional turbulence of the protagonist; the same gesture is used in movement 5, the other drinking song of the cycle. (2) In the "leitmotivic" manner fully developed by Wagner, Mahler repeatedly uses motives both to adumbrate and to recall other moments of the movement (and occasionally of the work), thereby enhancing its dramatic power and coherence.

In meter, tempo, and character – *schwungvoll*, as one early reviewer noted[14] – this music evokes a Viennese waltz gone awry as well as the driving triple-time of the *Eroica*. The tonal orientation lurches unsteadily between the two principal centers of the entire cycle, A (at the opening) and C (fig. 2–2), only to slip into B♭ with the entrance of the soloist, then back to A at his first cadence (fig. 4), and again up to B♭ for the highpoint of "The song of sorrow shall laughing in your soul *resound* [*klingen*]" (fig. 6). "Klingen" brings the piercing ring of the glockenspiel, which accents a variant on the basic pentatonic cell; the ensuing four bars markedly foreshadow the refrain and simultaneously highlight its close relation to the basic cell (cf. also Ex. 3[c] and R).

The crest of the line "welkt hin und *stirbt*" (fig. 9) introduces another element – "*y*" in Fig. 2 and Ex. 3 – that returns strophically and assumes pivotal importance in the fusion of sonata and strophic procedures at the approach to the reprise. In each case the gnashing dissonance underscores crucial words of the text: "dries up and *dies* the joy . . ." in the first strophe, "worth more than *all* the kingdoms . . ." in the second (fig. 22). Indeed, it is virtually an atonal sonority: 4–Z29 in pitch class set nomenclature (one of two forms of the all-interval tetrachord).[15] This is the sort of sound shortly to become standard vocabulary for Schoenberg and his followers; Mahler's underlying pedal point is chiefly responsible for pulling the chord back to a tonal context. But as Ex. 3(c) also shows, the *y* sonority derives as well from the "Japanese" (hemitonic) pentatonic scale *Hirajoshi*. So, too, does the refrain itself.[16]

The cadence to the first refrain is elided in Wagnerian style (the voice comes to rest on the tonic as the orchestra moves ahead), which immediately precipitates the instrumental introduction to the second exposition-*cum*-strophe. This is slightly longer and notably less stable in tonal function than the parallel music of the movement's opening; nevertheless, by way of C (mixed in mode, with added sixths, fig. 13 ff.) and B♭ (fig. 14 + 5 ff.), the tonic of A is resumed for the singer's first cadence in this new strophe. Thereafter follows another expansion: the previous foreshadowing of the refrain in B♭ (at "klingen") blossoms into an ironic twofold presentation of it – as counterpoint above the sung text, "To strike the lute and empty the glasses, those are the things that go well together" (figs. 18 and 19 ff.). As noted above, the modulatory scheme of this second exposition brings the refrain back a semitone higher (A♭ minor, fig. 23 + 5). It contains another noteworthy variant as well – the unusual chromatic stress of the article before the last word, "*der* Tod." One might dismiss this as clumsy text setting but for the Austrian and Bavarian custom of referring to people in conversation by surname plus article (e.g., cab drivers who spied the opera director on the street murmured to each other, "Der Mahler!").[17] Thus is Death, "der Tod," personified. A bittersweet orchestral echo follows, *pianissimo* and largely major in mode, which serves as transition to the development.

The development is also bipartite, in several respects. It is bisected by the onset of the third strophe (fig. 31–2 ff.), which overlaps the reprise. And the initial, purely instrumental interlude of the development is binary as well, articulated by the English horn motive and the two deceptive F minor cadences (figs. 25 and 28). All of the components here are closely related to music we have already heard (including the third-related tonal polarity of F minor and A♭, which is pentatonically derived). But the character of the material has been subtly yet fundamentally transformed, from agitated angst to uneasy tranquility and reflectiveness. Moreover, the two episodes of this interlude are premonitory; the melodic peaks of both (figs. 27 + 5 ff., 30 ff.) and the sequential descent of the second (fig. 29 ff.) softly adumbrate the crisis looming over the entire movement since the opening bars. Thus, the interlude's emphasis on polarities is not merely formal; rather, this portion of the *Trinklied* is a microcosm of syzygial oppositions inherent in the work as a whole. Leitmotivic association in the return of the voice clarifies that the reflective character of the development is an anticipation of "Der Abschied": the singer quietly intones "Das Firmament blaut ewig [The firmament blues eternally]" on the same three-step descending scale contour central to the ecstatic close of the finale, where the text is "Die liebe Erde allüberall blüht auf im Lenz und grünt auf's neu! [The beloved earth all over everywhere blooms forth in spring and greens up anew!]" (fig. 58 ff.; cf. Ex. 8 below). To underscore the foreshadowing, Mahler altered the Bethge text of the first movement (fig. 32 + 4): "und aufblüh'n im Lenz [and bloom forth in spring]" is his own interpolation, clearly alluding to "Der Abschied." But the anticipated transformation is not to occur here. The provisional calm in this grim drinking song is shattered by greater turmoil than heretofore: the strophic course of the music resumes and the singer, amidst acrid heterophonic clashes, bitterly demands, "Du aber, Mensch, wie lang lebst denn *du*? [But you, oh man, how long then live *you*?]" as the pungent dissonance of element *y* approaches for the third time (fig. 35 + 2 ff.). The crisis erupts in the scornful response, "Not even a hundred years," and with the melodic lurch of "dem morschen Tande dieser Erde! [the decaying trifles of this earth!]" the musical syntax verges on chaos, shot through with atonal and whole-tone sonorities.

At a stroke the recapitulation is underway: e^3/e^2 in the glockenspiel is the shortest dominant preparation in all of symphonic literature (fig. 39 - 1 ff.). Now the basic cell and its aftermath are texted for the first time (fig. 40 + 3 ff.), and the terror animating the movement's opening is at last explicitly identified: "In the moonlight, on the graves, crouches a wildly ghostlike form." The mock-heroic character of the head-motive horn fanfare (X) is revealed as well: "Hear you, how his howling shrieks forth in the sweet fragrance of *life*! [*Lebens*!]" The texture becomes frenetically heterophonic here,[18] and "Lebens" (fig. 44) is the raging climax of the entire movement, precipitating the most drastic of the melodic collapses characteristic of the whole: after bellowing his highest note, bb^1, for four bars, the tenor then drops in futility down a ninth as the orchestra tumbles yet farther, through pentatonic and whole-tone scales, to dominant preparation of A – the last of the reeling B♭–A tonal juxtapositions in this song (but not in *Das Lied* as a whole). Finally, having now heard "The Drinking Song of Earth's Sorrow," we are exhorted to seize and drain our glasses: "Dark is life, dark is death."

The presentation of the refrain is again twofold, although now the orchestra leads, in major, and the singer overlaps, in minor. But his cadence on "Tod" sets off the howling of the ape yet again, much as it had at the lunge into the second exposition: is this the coda, or will the movement unfold again? (Ironically, the first-movement coda of the *Eroica*, a great favorite of Mahler's, poses the same question.) But the commotion is arrested on a leitmotivic recall of "Leben" ($b\hat{6}$–$\hat{5}$, 49 + 1 ff.), then abruptly cut off by a dull tonic thud in the lowest register. Just as in the *Eroica* (and other symphonic predecessors), the movement's bristling energy has by no means been discharged, nor its conflict resolved, at the closing chord: resolution will require the remainder of the work, and especially the finale.

"Der Einsame im Herbst" ("The Lonely One in Autumn")

"The splendor of immediate life reflected in the medium of memory" is Adorno's brilliant aperçu about much of Mahler's late music.[19] Although the premonitory passages of the first movement manifest traces of such procedures, we first encounter them fully in the second song of *Das Lied* (possibly the first of the cycle to be composed).[20] Here the symbolic and dynamic polarity is between the inexorable transition of autumn (the present season) toward frozen winter, and the recurring bittersweet recollections of a summer warmth never to be felt again. The two main musical ideas embody these central poetic images in a complex, continuously developing dialogue, against the backdrop of a simple formal scheme – Specht's "rondo of falling leaves" – whereby the glow of the second idea emerges midway through each four-line strophe.

The raucous nocturnal drinking bout has been left far behind. Although the score calls for alto rather than tenor, Mahler's change in gender of the pronoun in the title – from "Die Einsame" (feminine) to "Der" (masculine) – underscores that the protagonist is the same, but now contemplates life from a different domain of the soul, standing alone on the edge of a lake. The song's primary material captures the mood projected onto the landscape, in the tradition of so many Romantic lieder. A languidly undulating violin ostinato in D minor imitates the rippling water and weaving laurel stems,[21] while the familiar pentatonic cell (d^2–c^2–a^1) in the solo oboe, now in slow motion, indeed sounds "somewhat furtive" and "weary," as the performance instructions indicate (*Etwas schleichend. Ermüdet*). The unpredictable chiaroscuro of the oboe line, the static pedal points, and the frequently heterophonic, chamber-like textures evoke drifting mists and shady reflections on the surface of the water. And this music is mildly exotic owing to a new device, the Chinese heptatonic scale (see Ex. 5; the pattern is like the Lydian mode, but without octave duplication). As he does with the pentatonicism of other movements, Mahler subjects the heptatonic idea to manifold variation and uses it to blur harmonic focus, often by rooting the seven-note scale pattern on a pitch other than the local tonic. The

Example 5   (a) heptatonic scale on F (= Lydian mode) (b) heptatonic scale on
Bb (c) heptatonic line from the ritornello of mvt. 2 (fig. 1 ff.) (d) heptatonic
sonority in the accompaniment

listless concave curves of the vocal line, which become virtually an ostinato in their own right, are a contour inversion of the restlessly rising and
tumbling lines that dominate the opening *Trinklied*. This music sounds
indeed as though "an artist had sifted jade powder" over the whole; it is a
tranquil yet vaguely foreign landscape.

The contrasting idea in Bb emerges in the horn (fig. **5**−2), "flowing,
molto espressivo, nobly sung" according to the score, with rich counterpoint in the cellos. Both of these lines are related to the foregoing
material, but their tone is far warmer: gone are the chilly heptatonic
scales and rippling ostinatos, replaced by lush appoggiaturas and chromaticism. Like several crucial passages of the first movement, this music
will be texted only near the end of the song (fig. **17** ff.), where we learn
the hitherto silent wish that prompts such glowing memory: "Der
Herbst in meinem Herze währt zu lange . . . [The autumn in my heart is
lasting too long]." But this is quickly suppressed in the first strophe, and
the ostinato returns, followed by hushed wailing winds in parallel
motion (fig. **6** ff.).

In the second strophe the contrasting swatch of Bb is longer and more
richly scored (fig. **9**–3ff.); this time the singer lapses into the rather dis-
tracted thought that "Soon the dried-up golden petals of the lotus blossoms will be floating on the water." During her ensuing silence the
orchestra weaves a new variant from the familiar fabric, music marked
"delicately urgent, tenderly passionate" (fig. **10**): in retrospect we realize
this is a distinct foreshadowing of the song's climax. But its energy

dwindles; D minor returns (fig. **11**), and the singer declares, literally "without expression [*ohne Ausdruck*]," "My heart is tired." Immediately the violins echo the chilly ascending contour of her first entry, wordlessly singing "covered with frost is all the grass." Her little lamp has gone out sparking, which commends her to sleep: B♭ returns briefly (fig. **12 + 1**) in a passage Adorno must have had in mind in observing that "The color of 'Der Einsame im Herbst,' the apotheosis of the orchestra of the *Kindertotenlieder*, is that of 'old gold.'"[22] And this in turn brings the transformation of the tonic D to the major mode (fig. **13**), where *Todessehnsucht* breaks through with the text "I come to you, beloved resting place, yes, give me rest . . .," the passage Webern considered "the pinnacle of music,"[23] which further foreshadows the highpoint.

That much-awaited fulfillment field emerges midway through the final strophe in an ecstatic semitone upsurge to E♭, as the singer finally reveals her longing for passionate warmth: "Sun of love, will you never more shine . . ." – but even now the violins remind her that she has already acknowledged "I come to you . . ." The answer to her question is self-evident, and D minor has returned before the final words of it, "mild aufzutrocknen? [tenderly to dry up?]," are expressionlessly uttered. As inexorably as before, the violins intone the wordless answer: "covered with frost is all the grass."

"Von der Jugend" ("Of Youth")

In the third and fourth songs the perspective shifts entirely to the past, in slightly wistful recollection of life stages gone by. Autumn is forgotten; these are songs of bright summer sunshine. In Adorno's view,

> in youth infinitely much is apprehended as a promise of life, as anticipated happiness, of which the ageing person recognizes, through memory, that in reality the moments of such promise were life itself. The missed and lost possibility is rescued by the very late Mahler, by contemplating it through the inverted opera glass of childhood, in which it might still have been possible. Those moments are designated by the choice of the poems of the third, fourth, and fifth songs.[24]

Richard Specht, however, believes that "the spectator is already beyond this world";[25] whether or not one agrees with that perspective, there is certainly, as he notes, a genial benevolence in the presentation of these vignettes.

The titles of these pieces, which are Mahler's own, probably adopt the formula "Von der . . ." from Nietzsche's *Also sprach Zarathustra*,[26] which proceeds in series of short chapters, each of which encapsulates (often ironically) a particular issue or viewpoint in the style of an expanded aphorism. "Von der Jugend" is the lightest and shortest of all the symphony's movements, and the most transparent in its *chinoiserie*; "Leicht und phantastisch [Light and fantastic]" was Mahler's provisional tempo marking in the piano autograph. It is indeed "Chinese rococo" in style, and comes closest to the function of a scherzo, as several reviewers of the premiere noted. And here, as well as in the following movement, some writers detect the influence of turn-of-the-century *Jugendstil* (*art nouveau* in France), with its emphasis upon stylization, delicate ornamentation, miniaturization, and flowing curves.[27] All of this is in marked contrast to what has gone before. But perhaps the most striking shift of polarities in "Von der Jugend" is the treatment of the voice: the virulent Dionysian heldentenor of the opening *Trinklied* must become a lyric singer of delicate Apollonian charm; the interplay of opposites continues.

The text describes sophisticated, carefree youths chatting animatedly, drinking tea, scribbling down verses, all in a green-and-white porcelain pavilion surrounded by water, and connected to *terra firma* only by the arching jade footbridge. Mahler captures this stylized atmosphere on the immediate surface of the music through pentatonic and whole-tone configurations. In addition, the texture is homophonic and treble-oriented, with prominent high flutes, fleeting ornaments, and perpetually chattering quavers animating the piece almost constantly: all of these features are virtually clichés derived from oriental music. As Arthur Wenk has observed, the arching contour of the bridge becomes the arch form of the song.[28] The seven stanzas of text are grouped 2 + 3 + 2 into a simple ABA format in which the principal tonality is B♭ and the modulatory scheme forms an arch of third-relations, B♭–G–E(major/minor)–G(minor/major)–B♭. Moreover, Mahler emphasizes this semicircular shape by inverting the order of Bethge's last two stanzas – what were originally nos. 6 and 7 are now 7 and 6 respectively. The upshot is "in my end is my beginning": the little piece concludes with the young people chatting and sipping endlessly, just as when it began.

This is Mahler's ironic comment on youthful insouciance, but the arch form also highlights his special treatment of the only potentially serious moment in either poetry or music: "and yet, the 'reflection'??!" as Webern quizzically referred to it.[29] The G minor strophe of the middle section (fig. 10 ff.) is not only "Ruhiger [calmer]," but indeed pensive: "on the pond's still, smooth surface everything shows up wonderfully in mirror image." Webern's tentative interpretation, that "youth sees things turned the wrong way" is certainly plausible, if inconclusive. Just what is revealed by the reflection? In response to this moment the orchestra grinds to a halt with faltering offbeats, as though the gramophone's spring had just wound down midway through a march or polka (fig. 13 ff.).[30] But by changing the order of poetic stanzas Mahler makes light of it all, in a ploy anticipating the more vigorous, even tragic denial of "The Drunkard in Springtime." By launching directly into the gaily chattering reprise with the line "Everything is standing on its head in the pavilion of green and white porcelain . . .," he makes the distorted images seem no more serious than those of a funhouse. The friends gossip on, and the music evaporates on a high $^6_4$ chord "like a transparent mirage [that] calls to mind the Chinese tale of the painter who vanishes into his picture . . .," as Adorno puts it. But he also reads more into this:

> Diminution, disappearance is the guise of death, in which music still preserves the vanishing. "Friends, beautifully dressed, drinking, talking" never really do so as in the miniature of memory, which promises that to the unborn. In such rejuvenation the dead are our children.[31]

And he suggests further psychological links between this song and "The Drunkard in Spring," as noted below.

"Von der Schönheit" ("Of Beauty")

In the fourth song the scene shifts from the artificial pavilion in the center of the pond to a riverbank for bittersweet reflection on youth's erotic awakening. The alto soloist resumes; as did the tenor in "Von der Jugend," she now presents a perspective on life altogether different from that of her first song. The commingled tenderness, desire, and uncertainty of the girl picking lotus blossoms seems almost Proustian, as

Adorno suggests.[32] "Absolute loveliness" and charming sweetness characterize her opening music, as Webern wrote to Berg.[33] But beneath this placid surface flows a Dionysian current that erupts in a thrilling show of power by the boys on horseback, the girl's secret beloved among them. This dialectic is central to the song, not only in the contrasts within its ternary form, but also in the striking thematic transformation spanning its principal sections that both unites and differentiates its feminine and masculine polarities, as Richard Specht recognized even at the work's premiere.[34] Nevertheless, the piece remains highly stylized and delicately elusive, like the recollection of time long past.

Mahler's textual alterations highlight the poem's erotic aspect: "Sonne spiegelt ihre schlanken Glieder [Sunlight mirrors their slender limbs]" and "Schmeichelkosen [cajoling caresses]" are his rather sensuous retouchings to Bethge's second stanza. And the original third stanza has been divided in two and expanded. This enables Mahler to emphasize the hot energy of the spirited horse, a traditional male symbol, in lines such as:

> Weithin glänzend wie die Sonnenstrahlen;
> [Gleaming into the distance like the rays of the sun]
> ....
>
> Über Blumen, Gräser wanken hin die Hufe,
> [Over flowers, grass, the hooves are scudding]
> ....
>
> hei! wie flattern im Taumel seine Mähnen,
> dampfen heiß die Nüstern!
> [ho! how his mane flaps in the frenzy,
> how hot his nostrils steam!]

Other details enhance this effect as well.[35] In the closing stanza of the song, it is Mahler who underscores the heated longing – *Sehnsucht* – in the girl's glances:

> In dem Funkeln ihrer großen Augen,
> in dem Dunkel ihres heißen Blicks
> [In the sparks of her large eyes,
> in the darkness of her hot glance]

And his revisions of the final line highlight both the nonfulfillment and enduring memory of her desire. Whereas Bethge had penned only

Figure 3   "Von der Schönheit," formal outline

Form		Tonality	Strophe	Text
A		G		Introduction
	a	G	1	Junge Mädchen pflücken Blumen . . .
	b	G		Zwischen Büschen und Blättern sitzen sie . . .
	a′	G	2	Gold'ne Sonne webt um die Gestalten . . .
	c	E; to $^V/_E$ ‖		Sonne spiegelt ihre schlanken Glieder . . .
B		G to C		Interlude, developmental
	d	C	3	O sieh, was tummeln sich für schöne Knaben . . .
		A♭/c		Interlude, wildly developmental
	d	F; D ‖	4	Das Roß des einen wiehert fröhlich auf . . .
A′	a′	B♭	5	Gold'ne Sonne webt um die Gestalten . . .
	c′	G		Und die schönste von den Jungfrau'n sendet . . .
	b	G		In dem Funkeln ihrer großen Augen . . .
		G		Postlude

"Wehklagt die Erregung ihres Herzens [The agitation of her heart laments]," Mahler is more specific: "Schwingt klagend noch die Erregung ihres Herzens nach [The agitation of her heart still reverberates plaintively within her]."

The reworking of the poem yields five stanzas of unequal length that Mahler disposes into a broad ABA′ format, with orchestral interludes between the third and fourth stanzas, as summarized in Figure 3. The song's tonal scheme accentuates the growing excitement and ensuing wistfulness of this reminiscence: each of the modulations arrives unexpectedly, and the music settles back into the tonic only after the thematic (and poetic) reprise has begun, thereby reflecting the still reverberating agitation of the girl's heart.

The character of the primary material ("A") partially resembles a minuet, as Specht notes, but it differs from the ancient dance movement in its vacillating meter and supple yet unpredictable phrase lengths. Once again, a delicate wash of pentatonicism suffuses the musical texture borne aloft in the upper winds, avoiding the gravity of the bass range. As the girls gather lotus blossoms into their laps (fig. 2 ff.), the rocking accompaniment of the violins recalls both the closing lullaby of the *Kindertotenlieder* ("they rest as though in their mother's house") and the nostalgic Andante of the Sixth Symphony. And the Zephyr's sensuous wafting of the girls' perfume finds precedent in Mahler's meditation on the fragrance of love from the souvenir of a linden branch, "Ich atmet' einen linden Duft [I breathed a delicate scent]," an earlier exploration of pentatonic exoticism (summer 1901).

The lads lustily invade this idyllic scene with what is arguably "the best horse music ever written," as music theorist David Lewin puts it.[36] There is a touch of ironic hyperbole in its military splendor as Mahler quotes Tchaikovsky's *1812 Overture* for a bar (fig. 8), and one senses more than a bit of parody in the Lisztian transformation of previous thematic material (see Ex. 6) – Mahler deployed this procedure only sparingly throughout his works, and was generally not fond of Liszt's orchestral music. Nevertheless, the raw power of both this and the succeeding orchestral interlude convincingly clinches his point about the dual nature of erotic *Sehnsucht*. A long incremental increase in tempo is called for throughout the entire "B" section, from "allmählich belebend [becoming animated by degrees]" just after fig. 7 through "Immer noch drängender [always still more pressing]" at fig. 15 + 1.

The second interlude is far wilder, and reveals Mahler *au courant* while very much on his own path. Both linearly and vertically, the musical frenzy here is controlled by a tonal mixture of A♭ and C minor in a manner that is virtually bitonal: related moments are to be found in Strauss's *Salome* (1905), which Mahler had fought hard, albeit unsuccessfully, to premiere in Vienna. Nevertheless, this seeming chaos is also developmental in the manner Mahler so prized: the kernel of the A♭/C mixture is the hemitonic (Japanese) pentatonic scale *Hirajoshi*, and verticalizations of *Kumoijoshi* are also frequent (see Ex. 3 above). Whole-tone and "ordinary" pentatonic fragments provide additional spice. The alienating capacity of the work's exoticism has been pressed to new extremes; here, as in the approach to the reprise of "Das Trinklied vom Jammer der Erde," Mahler's music draws close to the exaggeration and distortion of Expressionism.

By the end of the fourth strophe the singer is, designedly, almost as breathless as the horse she sings about.[37] Then in an instant the

Example 6 Thematic transformation in mvt. 4: (a) bars 1–3 and 7–9 (b) fig.
8+1 ff.

uproarious cavalcade vanishes and the reprise is at hand (fig. 16) via
another of the abrupt modulations (here D → B♭ by way of V of B) that
have become almost motivic. It is as though the album leaf were suddenly
flipped – an ineluctable indication that the horse episode is, in Adorno's
phrase, "the splendor of immediate life reflected in the medium of
memory." But the girl's ardent longing remains, now linked through
musical recollection with the caress of the Zephyr. For Adorno her
glance is the glance of *Das Lied* as a whole, "absorbing, doubting, turned
backwards with precipitous tenderness . . . like the gaze of Proust's
Recherche . . ." In the tradition of Schumann's *Dichterliebe*, the instrumental postlude is as expressive and arresting as all that preceded it.

Audience and singer remain suspended in reflection upon what is ur solved, and like "Von der Jugend," the song fades ethereally in the instability of a high tonic $^6_4$. Adorno's insightful and provocative commentary on this moment is worth citing in extenso:

> The end of "Von der Schönheit," the clarinet entry in the epilogue [upbeat to fig. 21 + 5], a passage the like of which is granted to music only every hundred years, rediscovers time as irrecoverable. In both [i.e., Proust and Mahler] unfettered joy and unfettered melancholy perform their charade; in the prohibition of images of hope, hope has its last dwelling-place. This place is in both, however, the strength to name the forgotten that is concealed in the stuff of experience. Like Proust, Mahler rescued his idea from childhood. In that his idiosyncratically unmistakable, unexchangeable aspect nevertheless became universal, the secret of all, he surpasses all of the music of his time; in this he was probably equaled among composers only by Schubert.[38]

"Der Trunkene im Frühling" ("The Drunk in Spring")

The next vignette, fifth song of the cycle, is also its second drinking song. Yet it is, once again, a polar contrast – not only to the immediately preceding movement for alto, but also to both of the tenor's previous offerings. Mahler himself drank only sparingly. Yet as his first letter to Bruno Walter from the summer of *Das Lied* reveals, he had come to realize that his own opiate was work: "over the course of the years I have forgotten how to do anything else. It's as though I were a morphine addict or a drunkard to whom one forbade his vice all at once."[39] This closing movement of the symphony's first *Abteilung* is a searing satire of frivolous intoxication, the flipside of the bitter cynicism in the first drinking song. Here the eerie cheeriness and denial of reality call to mind Schubert's "Täuschung" in *Winterreise* – "deception is my only prize." "Der Trunkene" is also a sardonic parody of Dionysian impotence. The reawakening of spring, season of great Dionysian festivals, is indeed at hand, yet the orgiastic cortège comprises but a single Bacchant – an ebullient buffoon who falls asleep on his doorstep every night and can't remember what season is at hand.

Yet there are affinities to the previous movements as well. "Der Trunkene im Frühling" is in a broad ternary format like "Von der Jugend" and "Von der Schönheit," and as in those songs, stylization distances us from the scene described, even as the singer is here separated from himself by drunkenness. Both the jingling eighths and the high wind sounds of *chinoiserie* are by now a commonplace background pattern. The mock-heroic pentatonic horn calls punctuated by accented trilling recall "Das Trinklied vom Jammer der Erde," as do the numerous lurching tonal shifts – especially A to B♭ in the "A" sections (e.g., bars 1–5, figs. 2–3 and 12–2 ff.). So, too, do the melodic contours in reeling arches, which suggest drinking to the limits of endurance (cf. figs. 1 and 10). And even more frequently than in the opening movement, the tenor line clashes tipsily against the orchestral fabric (e.g., figs. 4, 10, and 13).

The middle portion of this song, and especially the setting of "Aus tiefstem Schauen lauscht' ich auf [in deepest gazing I 'listened up'],'' deeply impressed at least two listeners at the premiere who knew Mahler personally. Webern considered this spot "the most enigmatic thing ever" and wanted to "give up the ghost" when he first heard it; Specht thought it "practically sums up his [Mahler's] being," and he also emphasizes the tragic aspect of its juxtaposition against "the almost exaggerated boisterousness and unruliness of all the rest."[40] To be sure, the passage is memorable in several respects: like the fifth strophe of "Von der Jugend," this is a moment of mysterious, sobering reflection. Yet here we know what about: spring, the eternal renewal of nature, which is to be apotheosized in the extraordinary conclusion of the work as a whole. For this is the second occurrence of this musical phrase, now in low tessitura and the unfamiliar tonal region of D♭; earlier it bore the text "Ich frag' ihn ob schon Frühling sei [I ask him if it's already spring]" (fig. 6 + 3 ff.). And beneath the surface is a self-quotation that will crop up in the finale as well: the minor-to-major chromatic passing motion from scale degree ♭$\hat{3}$ to $\hat{4}$ over pedal points strongly recalls "als sei kein Unglück" from the first of the *Kindertotenlieder* ("as though no misfortune had transpired during the night"; see Ex. 11 below) – indeed a Mahlerian leitmotif that "practically sums up his being."

Adorno contends that the literary point of the "reflection" episode in "Von der Jugend" is closely related to "Der Trunkene," and, moreover, reflects Mahler's own situation:

His situation is already the Expressionist one behind the mask of the objective ballad tone. The inner space is isolated, without a bridge to life, yet Mahler's music clings to life with every slender thread. With paradoxical realism the work thinks the situation through to the end, without glossing over anything: the affinity to Proust lies in the interior monologue. The sadness of the pond as a mirror is that for Weltschmerz, which finally cuts the threads, the allure of real life seems like the dream that the first line of the poem invokes, even while objectless inwardness is turning itself into reality, its opposite. When in a passage moving beyond all words the drunk [*der Trunkene*] hears the bird's voice, Nature as an exhortation of the earth, it is for him "as though in a dream." In vain would he go back once more. His loneliness somersaults in drunkenness between despair and joy of absolute freedom, already in the zone of death. The spirit of this music converges with that of Nietzsche, of whom Mahler was an adherent in his youth. But where the Dionysos of the objectlessly inward erects his tablets with imperious impotence, Mahler's music departs from hubris in that it still reflects its own cry, and composes into itself laughter about its untruth. The intoxication of self-destruction; the heart that cannot contain itself gives itself away to that from which it has departed. Its going under longs for reconciliation . . . But the reeling of the drunk, which the music imitates, lets death in through the gaps between tones and chords. In Mahler music overtakes the terror of Poe and Baudelaire, the *goût du néant* [taste for nothingness], as though it had become estrangement from one's own body.[41]

In any case, whatever has been grasped "in deepest gazing" becomes merely the pretext for filling and draining the cup yet again (fig. **10**). Such intoxicated denial – significantly proclaimed in C (major), one of the two principal tonalities of the symphony overall – becomes tragic irony in Mahler's hands, and prepares for "Der Abschied," just as Specht suggests. Meanwhile, the tonal reprise of A for the final strophe of "Der Trunkene" is decisive for both the movement's structure and symbolism. "What does spring matter to me?! Let me be drunk!" is the singer's parting shot, and the piece concludes with an uproarious flourish of A major that reverberates in the mind's ear long after its vibrations have ceased.

"Der Abschied" ("The Farewell")

"Death knell" (*Grabgeläute*) was Mahler's note to himself at the first entrance of the tam-tam in the short score of "Der Abschied" (see Plate 3). That sound had long been a sonic symbol of death for him, as for many of his predecessors.[42] Initially Mahler planned for the tam-tam to mark the midpoint of the broad two-part finale to his new work, as yet unnamed. Eventually he decided that strokes of the gong would punctuate the opening deep C pedal of "Der Abschied" as well – an icy quelling of the previous song in a gesture that brings us face to face with all that the drinker had sought to deny. In this farewell the polar oppositions and binary structurings of the entire work peak and dissolve. As Paul Bekker notes, it is an exceptional manifestation of the powerful pull towards the finale characteristic of the Mahlerian symphony (as also, for example, in the Fourth and Sixth):

> The first five songs lie like a multicolored garland of bright and dark sketches of life forming a circle around the last piece. The proclamation of farewell from life and the earth also retroactively gives them significance in their individual content and in their juxtaposition.[43]

Yet as suggested above, it also dissolves them. Throughout this movement the traditional processes of musical motion are blurred or liquidated, suggesting that ordinary time–space relations, or at least one's perception of them, are breaking down. So, too, is recollection of the past.

As we have seen, the Swiss critic William Ritter first hit upon the striking connection between the macrolevel binary structures of *Das Lied von der Erde* and the Eighth Symphony. In Part I of the Eighth, "Faust-Adam" boldly demands that the *creator spiritus* come down, whereupon in Part II he himself is drawn up into heaven by the divine mother. Similarly, in *Das Lied* both the first and last movements contain the appeal to Death as liberator – "a call ironic and terrible, philosophical and swaggering" in the first movement, but "resigned and tender, confident, imploring, and gentle" in the finale. "That is the basis of the work," writes Ritter, "which henceforth decomposes itself accordingly" – so successfully, indeed, that it is not altogether surprising to find the unsympathetic critic Rudolf Louis complaining after the premiere that the last movement is monotonous.[44]

Structurally this long finale is relatively simple, yet its form is by no means immediately apparent. Two adjacent poems from Bethge's *Die chinesische Flöte* form the textual basis of the movement's two halves: "In Expectation of the Friend" by Mong-Kao-Jen, and "Departure of the

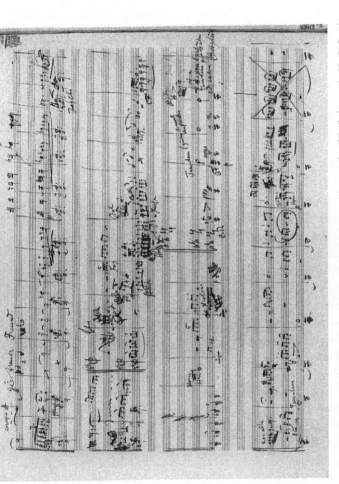

Plate 3 "Der Abschied," short score (*Particell*) corresponding to fig. 35–5 through 40–3. In the third system following the return to C minor, Mahler writes "Tam-tam (zum 1. mal auftreten [Tam tam enters for the first time]", and, near the right margin, "Grabgeläute [Death knell]." At the top of the page the singer's text is "[un–] getreuer Freund [faithless friend]," a line of Bethge's poem Mahler subsequently changed to "Lebens trunk'ne Welt [world drunken of life]."

Figure 4   "Der Abschied," formal scheme

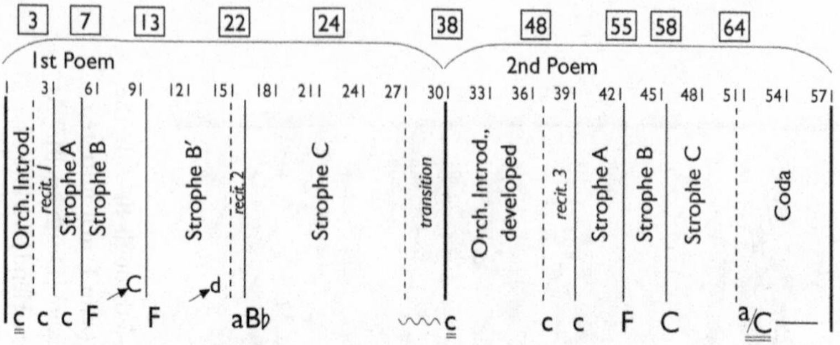

Friend" by Wang-Wei. According to Bethge, the two poets were writing to each other.[45] Mahler, however, made more alterations and interpolations in this pair of poems than in any other text of *Das Lied*, whereby, as Arthur Neisser observed following the work's premiere, the "friend" in question is none other than Freund Hain, the spectre of Death who appeared as an ape howling on the gravestones in the first movement (see the translation in the Appendix, where Mahler's changes are underlined). The purported dialogue between two poets thus becomes an interior monologue and, ultimately, the ecstatic fusion of Death with the persona represented by the singer.

Within the broad binary structure of "Der Abschied," as Robert Bailey has shown, three large musical sections or strophes are deployed, as indicated in Figure 4.[46] Each half of the movement opens with introductory orchestral material (considerably extended in the second part) and a recitative in C minor. In Part I the tonality then shifts to F for strophes B and B', followed by a second recitative in A minor, the other component of the work's fundamental A/C tonal pairing. Strophe C then arrives in the unexpected tonality of Bb, up a semitone from the recitative that introduces it. In Part II, strophe C recurs a further step higher, in C; overall, its rising pitch level is another manifestation of intensifying "expressive tonality" (cf. the threefold appearance of the first movement's refrain). Omission of strophe B' in Part II allows time for the finale's crucial coda, yet without disturbing the symmetry of its binary structure. (In Bruno Walter's third and last recording of *Das Lied von der Erde*, the two halves are balanced at 14'26" and 14'42" respectively.)[47]

Example 7   1–3 and 5, quasi-ostinato motives in mvt. 6; 4, Second
Symphony, finale, "The Bird of Death" (Fig. 31–5 ff.)

Nevertheless, symmetrical structure is not an immediately striking
facet of this finale, particularly by comparison with the taut brevity of
the first movement. Above all, "Der Abschied" is repetitious – in the
foreground, through the virtually endless recycling of ostinato-like
components, the chief of which are shown in Ex. 7. Eventually these
recurring motives seem to lose distinct identity, blurring into a static and
apparently endless background. They are intertwined by a subtle web of
relationships, yet only rarely (but then significantly) do these connec-
tions develop into distinctive musical events. At a broader level, the three
recitatives bring all regular motion to a halt, and the ensuing large
musical strophes (A, B, and C) seem static as well, making little or no
headway within or between themselves. In Part I each of these sections
builds toward a climax, only to collapse in gestures of disintegration

(figs. **4** + 6 to **7**; **10** + 5 through **13**; **14** to **18**; **33** to **38**). Repeatedly the local pulse of the music is blurred by cross rhythms (e.g., 5, 4, or 3 against 2, sometimes in multiple combinations), and also by related effects of heterophony – a general characteristic of Eastern music here deployed to impede our sense of forward motion.[48] Distinct phrase structures are largely avoided. And tonal direction is blurred as well – chiefly through pentatonicism, but also via whole-tone configurations and other sonorities approaching free atonality. Dominant preparation resulting in overt cadence is rare, and broad linear motion (the Schenkerian middleground) is often deflected.

All of these interrelated procedures project the gradual yet inexorable dissolution of normal musical time and space. As noted in Chapter 1, Mahler had first experimented with such techniques following his near-death experience of 1901, particularly in the Rückert lied "Ich bin der Welt abhanden gekommen [I have become lost to the world]" that represented for him a reunion with "my very self." Now comes the farewell to earth and the earthly self: no previous movement by Mahler is so fully and extensively focused on the immediate flow of inner feeling, on what remains of the present even as it slips away.

Part I: "In Expectation of the Friend"

Following the two ominous low Cs punctuated by tam-tam, the oboe sounds the first of four frequently recurring elements unveiled in the course of this brief instrumental introduction (Ex. 7–1): stylistically it resembles the *broderie* or traditional ornamentation of a simpler melody already familiar to European cognoscenti of Chinese music.[49] The second ostinato-like motive crystalizes slowly (Ex. 7–2[a]): this is the vague kernel of a march topos that will unfold with tragic solemnity in the orchestral interlude that opens Part II (cf. Ex. 7–2[b]).[50] But here, just as the motive begins to establish a regular pulse, the first minor–major modal shift takes place – a recurrent symbol of transition from darkness to light (or vice versa) throughout "Der Abschied." Next, in leitmotivic manner (fig. 2–2 ff.), the oboe adumbrates the singer's simile of the moon as a silver ship (fig. 4 + 6 ff.). But like the music it foreshadows, this luminous moment is quashed by the third frequently recurring motive, a scurrying chromatic flourish for high winds that will articulate many moments of collapse (Ex. 7–3); it is directly related to the flute accompaniment of the first two recitatives, and inevitably it calls to mind the "Bird of Death" heard after the Great Roll Call in the finale of Mahler's Second Symphony (Ex. 7–4). As this gesture fades away, the harps introduce yet another ostinato component (Ex. 7–2[c]) that will feature prominently in succeeding portions of the movement.

From this bewildering stasis emerges the initial recitative. As William Ritter observed, the movement evokes a striking alpine atmosphere.[51] Moreover, the scene set by the opening text and music – shadows of nightfall beside a mountain lake, bright moonlight, rustling pine trees – is virtually identical with the landscape in which Mahler revealed to Natalie the vivid dream of being summoned away by Death that had haunted him for nearly twenty years. It recalls as well Mahler's childhood memory of being abandoned in the woods, lost in reverie, as Alma Mahler noted.[52] In the course of "Der Abschied" chilly darkness, wind, water, and birds variously surface and fade from consciousness, yet this stylized collage never seems out of place; nor does it disrupt the deeper flow of inner consciousness, which is manifest through the extraordinary treatment of time and tonality.

The recitative introduces the first brief musical strophe (A), which, as noted, also disintegrates into silence. Now the recurring motives reemerge in the listless current of the brook (fig. **7**; cf. Ex. 7–1 and 5[a]), portrayed through remarkably heterophonic dissynchronization of lines; the key is F, the relaxed subdominant of C, the mode major, and a new section, Strophe B, is at hand. Here Mahler has modified the poetry to reveal in passing that it is spring ("The flowers pale in the twilight"), a fact that initially seems superfluous. But the orchestra soon blossoms into music (fig. **10** + 5 ff.) shortly to be allied with another of Mahler's own lines, "All longing [*Sehnsucht*] will now only dream" (fig. **14**) – the predominant theme of the entire work. Ecstatic, and tinged with exotic harmonies (several derived from whole-tone and half-diminished seventh sonorities), this gesture also plummets back to C minor (fig. **13**–2), followed directly by the onset of Strophe B′ (fig. **13**).[53]

This section begins as a condensed variation of Strophe B.[54] The "Sehnsucht" music arrives with text (fig. **14**), but its rapturous longing soon gives way to the uncertain pulse and darker C♯ minor tonality of "Die müden Menschen geh'n heimwärts . . . [the tired men go homeward]" (fig. **15** + 3 ff.). Melodically, this is a quotation of "Mein Herz ist müde [my heart is tired]" and "mild aufzutrocknen [gently to dry up [my bitter tears]]" from "Der Einsame im Herbst." But the text, and specifically the ensuing line "um im Schlaf vergess'nes Glück und Jugend neu zu lernen! [to learn anew in sleep forgotten happiness and youth!]," alludes to one of the passionate and melancholy poems Mahler had written in December 1884 for the projected six songs of his *Lieder eines fahrenden Gesellen* (*Songs of a Wayfarer*), which he privately dedicated to the singer Johanna Richter during the breakup of their amorous liaison:[55]

> Die Nacht blickt mild aus stummen, ew'gen Fernen
> Mit ihren tausend goldnen Augen nieder –
> Und müde Menschen schließen ihre Lider,
> Im Schlaf auf's Neu', vergess'nes Glück zu lernen!
>
> Siehst du den stummen fahrenden Gesellen?
> Gar einsam und verloren ist sein Pfad . . .
>
> [The night looks gently down from silent, everlasting heavens
> With her thousand golden eyes
> And tired men close their eyelids
> In sleep anew to learn forgotten happiness
>
> Do you see the silent wayfarer?
> Quite lonely and forsaken is his path . . .]

There is no star to light the wayfarer's path, no rest in sight, no answer to the riddles of the sphinx – such, evidently, were Mahler's associations with this passage of "Der Abschied," which lend it the quality of youthful promise reflected in memory that Adorno finds so compelling in late Mahler. An all-too-noisy flock of birds breaks into this bittersweet nostalgia (fig. 18 + 3 ff.), only to be silenced by the recurring gesture of Ex. 7–3, now an ominous sort of bird call in the lower register. As the world falls asleep ("Die Welt schläft ein"), musical motion once again ceases, underscoring the traditional symbolic affiliation of sleep and death.

The onset of the A minor recitative is a regression to the movement's beginning, but (as noted above) in the other polarity of the work's third-related key areas (A and C). Here the singer reveals, in a line Mahler added, the reason for this nocturnal vigil – "I stand here awaiting my friend. I await his last farewell." And we realize what is so ominous about the pine grove: thence will come Freund Hain. Then the focus of consciousness shifts yet again, and the ensuing orchestral interlude that

Example 8   "Der Abschied," the "Erde" or "ewig" motive in first and
subsequent appearances.
(Texts: **58**, "The beloved earth . . ."; **62**, "blue brightly the horizons . . ."; **64**,
"Eternally, ever . . .")

opens Strophe C (fig. **24** ff.) is a bright contrast in meter (3/4), key (B♭),
and flowing motion (*Fließend*, gradually becoming one beat per bar) to
all that has gone before. The ostinatos (Ex. 7–5 [b] and [c]) become
lilting, the texture is delicately suffused with pentatonicism, and there
emerges a broad melody later fully associated with "Die liebe Erde [the
beloved earth]" and the ecstatic release of spirit into the cosmos; its
second phrase is the famous "Ewigkeit" motive that crops up repeatedly
in Mahler (see Ex. 8, and cf. Ex. 1).[56] Anxiety is temporarily forgotten,
and by the time of the singer's second line of text, "die Schönheit dieses
Abends zu genießen [to enjoy the beauty of this evening]," the music
seems to quiver in anticipation of the coming encounter with eternity.

The Dionysian high point of this strophe, and indeed of the finale's
first half, surges forth in a minor–major thrust toward C (fig. **34** + 3 ff.).
The text is Mahler's – "O Schönheit! O ewigen Liebens, Lebens trunk-
'ne Welt! [O Beauty! O world drunken of eternal love-and-life!]" – yet it

Example 9   (a) Recurring motive prominent in the instrumental interlude of mvt. 6, fig. **39** ff. (b) its relation to the opening recitative (text: "The sun departs behind [the mountain . . .]") (c) its relationship to a prominent motive in Strophe B (text: "I wander [to and fro with my lute]"), fig. **26** ff., here at **30**+9.

could nearly be Faust's as well: "Then to the moment could I say: Linger you now, you are so fair!" Or Zarathustra's: "if you ever said 'You please me, happiness! Abide, moment!' then you wanted *all* back."[57] The wayfarer's passions are still of this earth; Mephistopheles may win his wager after all; yet all may recur eternally. This musical moment, which encapsulates all the longing and the richness of individuated will manifest and recalled during the first five movements of "The Song of the Earth," can no more be prolonged than any moment preceding it. Decisive musical collapse follows, bringing yet another regression to the state of the finale's opening: its midpoint is at hand.

Part II: "Departure of the Friend"

With the return of C minor (fig. **38**), the tam-tam, silent since the movement's introduction, begins its knell again. (It was here that Mahler made the annotation "Grabgeläute" in his short score [Plate 3].) Within bars (fig. **39**) a prominent "new" recurring motive appears: it is, however, derived from the shape of the recitative's opening (which, in turn, grew from the introductory motives), and is also related via rhythm and contour inversion to two other motives heard earlier (Ex. 9). Thus, a

Example 10   "einsam Herz" motive in "Der Abschied" (a) fig. **42**–1; (b) **44**–2; (c) **54**–1 ff. (Text: "Peace for my lonely heart . . .")

latent and sinister aspect of previously familiar music becomes predominant; the motive is particularly unnerving in the context of gnashing parallel tritones (the interval known to the ancients as *diabolus in musica*, the devil in music – fig. **40**–1 ff.). When next this melodic gesture is texted, the words will be: "Er stieg vom Pferd und reichte ihm den Trunk des Abschieds dar . . . [He dismounted from the horse and offered him the drink of farewell]" (fig. **48** + 1).

Meanwhile, the kernels of march music inherent in the movement's introduction flourish into a long funereal march, colored by wailing windband texture. Broadly "developmental," it makes no actual headway, and searing dissonances notwithstanding, never strays far from C minor. The only striking motivic evolution is the twofold adumbration of material later allied to the words "einsam Herz [lonely heart]" (figs. **42**–1 and **44**–2; see Ex. 10). Relentlessness is the chief characteristic of this inner vision of a march – funereal indeed, yet not for a funeral. As the procession comes to a grim halt the gong continues to toll, and we know who has arrived on a horse bearing the draught of departure (according to the Book of Revelation, it is to be a pale horse). But now Mahler deliberately alters the Bethge texts to blur the identity of the interlocutors through indiscriminate use of the third-person pronoun, "er" – "He stepped from the horse and offered him the draught . . . He asked him whither he led . . . He spoke . . .," etc. Inescapably, this suggests that the musical persona and the archetypal figure of Death have become one, inseparably fused, no longer adversaries.[58] The probable precedent for such a symbolic union is the love-death passage of *Tristan und Isolde* (Act II), in which the lovers anticipate complete dissolution of their individualities into total unity with each other: "I, Tristan," she sings, and "I, Isolde," he answers; "No more Isolde! no more Tristan! Without naming, without parting, to know anew, enkindled anew, eternally, endlessly!"

As we shall see, this provides a clue to the final outcome of *Das Lied*. But before that moment arrives, the modified reprise of Strophe A, which had initially set the scene in anticipation of Death's arrival, now provides an enigmatic answer to "why it had to be [*warum es müßte sein*]." The line is Mahler's own interpolation, but the question was most famously posed in music by Beethoven, as "The Difficult Decision [*Der schwer gefaßte Entschluß*]" in the epigraph to his last string quartet, Op. 135 ("Muß es sein? Es muß sein!"*)*. Mahler responds with unaltered words from Bethge, thereby remaining nearly as cryptic as Beethoven: "Fate was not favorable to me in this world!" (fig. 51 ff.). Yet the younger composer has left several hints about his veiled meaning. One thinks again of Faust, striving proudly and blindly to the very end: such labor had become Mahler's opiate, as he had revealed to Bruno Walter (cf. "O ewigen Liebens, Lebens trunk'ne Welt!"). And as noted, earlier in the movement Mahler makes a nostalgic allusion to his own past in declaiming that tired men shall learn anew in sleep their forgotten happiness. Now Strophe A' concludes (fig. 53 + 4 ff.) with an unmistakable reference to the first song of the *Kindertotenlieder*, composed the summer after the fateful events of 1901 (see Ex. 11). The misfortune of the night in "Nun will die Sonn' so hell aufgeh'n [Now Will the Sun as Brightly Rise]" was the death of a child – symbolically, the death of childlike trust and love, such as is manifest in Mahler's earlier works, most particularly "Das himmlische Leben [Heavenly Life]." Thus this nostalgic nocturnal moment in "Der Abschied" would seem to be a private expression of mourning near the end of life for innocence lost and utopian hope unfulfilled.

The reprise of Strophe B (fig. 55 ff.) is heavily condensed, which both balances the overall binary form after the long march-interlude that

Example 11 (a) *Kindertotenlieder*, No. 1, "Nun will die Sonn' so hell aufgeh'n [Now the sun will rise just as brightly]," bars 10–14, transposed (original: D minor) (b) *Das Lied von der Erde*, "Der Abschied," fig. **53** +4 ff. (Texts: [a] "as though no misfortune the night [had seen]" [b] "I go, I wander into the mountains. I seek peace, peace [for my lonely heart].")

inaugurates Part II, and hastens the finale's close. The voice enters almost immediately, and the first line of poetry is Mahler's: "Ich wandle nach der Heimat, meiner Stätte! [I wander homeward, to my abode!]" Peace is at last in view for the wanderer, the *fahrender Gesell* who had claimed he was thrice homeless. Just as the "Sehnsucht" music sounds in the orchestra (fig. **57**–4), the singer's words countermand it: "I shall nevermore roam afar. Still is my heart and awaits its hour!" And now time and tonality seem almost to evaporate; exotic scales ascend through a tritone up to E, slower in each instance, and whole-tone ambiguity suffuses the harmony.

The onset of C major is hardly to be expected; the ethereal e♮³ is the sole delicate fibre connecting what has been to what now transpires. The recurrence of Strophe C is formally logical (fig. **58**), but it now becomes undisturbed ecstasy of light, as temporal definition gradually recedes in the radiant pulsing of cross-rhythms and arpeggiation, scintillating with harps and celesta. The music of "O Schönheit! O ewigen Liebens, Lebens trunk'ne Welt!" is transformed to "und ewig, ewig blauen licht die Fernen [and ever, eternally, brightly blue the horizons]," and from fig. **63** on the texture is saturated with pentatonicism. The descending "ewig" motive (Ex. 8) is combined with the ascending arpeggiation of scale form *Yu* (fig. **64**), formerly sung to "Ich wandle auf und nieder mit meiner Laute [I wander to and fro with my lute]" (fig. **30** + 8 ff.: *Yu*, in

115

contour inversion, had been the basic cell of movement 1, "The Drinking Song of Earth's Sorrow" – cf. Ex. 3, fourth line). But at length B♮, leading tone to the tonic, is lost (after fig. **67–5**). The fusion of A and C becomes vertically established, and all other fleeting sonorities only highlight its permanence. The singer cadences briefly at fig. **65**, but the last three utterances of the ninefold "ewig" do not descend to c^1. As Benjamin Britten observed of this extraordinary close,

> It has the beauty of loneliness & of pain: of strength & freedom. The beauty of disappointment & never-satisfied love. The cruel beauty of nature, and everlasting beauty of monotony.
> ... And there is nothing morbid about it ... a serenity literally supernatural. I cannot understand it – it passes over me like a tidal wave – and that matters not a jot either, because it goes on forever, even if it is never performed again – that final chord is printed on the atmosphere.[59]

Therewith Mahler prescinds from resolving the poetic–musical polarities of his art, but simply merges them at the moment of liminal transition. One can read this valediction from several perspectives that influenced his thought and work. The concluding lines of the text are Mahler's own (except for "I will never more wander ..."):

> I wander to the homeland, to my abode!
> I will never more wander afar.
> Still is my heart, and awaits its hour!
>
> The beloved earth all over everywhere
> Blossoms forth in spring and greens up anew!
> Everywhere and ever brightly blue the horizons,
> Eternally ... ever ...

Both poetry and music here bear striking affinity to Fechner's view that death is simply the transition to the third stage of existence, that of eternal waking; therefore we really have no reason to fear it any more than the trauma of birth from the womb.[60] Fechner also teaches that people make for themselves the conditions of their future lives, and that the soul continues to develop after death "according to the unalterable law of nature upon earth"[61] (a view Mahler espoused in conversation with Richard Specht).[62] For Fechner, the transition to eternal waking is a rapturous release:

our future life will merge as one with waves of light and sound . . .

The spirit will no longer wander over mountain and field, or be surrounded by the delights of spring, only to mourn that it all seems exterior
to him; but, transcending earthly limitations, he will feel new strength and
joy . . .

Stilled is all restlessness of thought, which no longer needs to seek in order
to find itself . . .

when man dies, . . . as the waves roll forth into the sea of ether and the sea
of air, he will not merely feel the blowing of the wind and the wash of the
waves against his body, but will himself murmur in the air and sea; no
more wander outwardly through verdant woods and meadows, but
himself consciously pervade both wood and meadow and those wandering there.[63]

Thus, colors can indeed become verbs in Mahler's final lines of "Der
Abschied"; spatio-temporal distinctions no longer obtain.

As noted in Chapter 3, Richard Specht's review of the premiere asso-
ciates the close of "Der Abschied" with the ecstatic musical rhetoric of
Isolde's Transfiguration at the conclusion of *Tristan*. So, too, does the
letter from Britten just quoted in part, and drawing upon that source,
Donald Mitchell briefly concurs. More recently, Hermann Danuser has
suggested, with little elaboration, that the close of "Der Abschied"
"brings the symphonic process to its inevitable conclusion, while at the
same time lending it a necessary degree of that unending quality inherent in the *Weltanschauung* model of a love/death dialectic."[64] Other listeners have made the same observation independently. Yet there is an
inherent puzzle: on the surface, neither the existential situation nor
Mahler's poetry seems related to the realm of the erotic, whereas Isolde's
Transfiguration music inevitably carries associations of erotic longing
and ecstasy, precisely because it is the reprise and resolution of the inter-
rupted love duet in Act II of *Tristan*.

In the Schopenhauerian worldview, Eros and Thanatos hold the
balance as mutual conditions of each other; Shiva bears both the necklace of skulls and the *lingam*. From this broader perspective, the musical
overtones of Tristanesque ecstasy in "Der Abschied" are indeed an
appropriate subtext to the lines being sung. And from a practical stand-
point, it is difficult to imagine what other musical precedent Mahler

could have drawn upon to convey such a climactic moment of transition. As we have seen, he had earlier deployed the love/death dialectic following his life-threatening illness in 1901: music deeply associated both with maternal love and with "dying away entirely" at the threshold of Paradise in the Fourth Symphony became "my very self, lost to the world" in "Ich bin der Welt abhanden gekommen," and was subsequently transformed into the rapturous Adagietto of the Fifth, reportedly a declaration of love for Alma.[65]

Stuart Feder makes the equally intriguing suggestion that, from the psychoanalytic perspective, "Der Abschied" resembles a "reunion fantasy" of return to the maternal security of the womb – another facet of the birth–death polarity.[66] Such feelings were not unknown to Mahler: in a long and frequently cited "literary" letter of his youth to his friend Joseph Steiner, Mahler laments: "O my much-beloved earth, ah when will you take the forsaken one into your womb [*in deinen Schoß*] . . . he flees . . . to you, to you! O, receive the lonely one, him who is without peace, all-eternal mother!!"[67] And in the autograph manuscript of the *Kindertoten-lieder*, he had revised the last line of the cycle's text to read "They rest as if in their mother's womb [*Schoß*]," rather than Rückert's "in their mother's house," which he ultimately restored in the *Stichvorlage*.[68]

But it is Nietzsche near the end of *The Birth of Tragedy*, a central work in Mahler's maturation, who combines all of the foregoing symbols in an extraordinary passage Mahler cannot have missed:

> The *tragic myth* is to be understood only as a symbolization of Dionysian wisdom through Apollinian artifices. The myth leads the world of phenomena to its limits where it denies itself and seeks to flee back again into the womb [*in den Schoß*] of the true and only reality, where it then seems to commence its metaphysical swansong, like Isolde:[69]

And here Nietzsche quotes the close of her Transfiguration:

> In the sea of rapture's
> surging swell,
> in the scented waves'
> resounding knell,
> in the vast world-breath's
> billowing All –
> to drown – sink down –
> unconscious – supremest bliss!

In his next sentence Nietzsche concludes that the "vast Dionysian impulse" of the tragic artist "devours the entire phenomenal world" of his creative work, "in order to foreshadow, beyond it and through its destruction, the highest artistic primal joy, in the womb of the primordial Oneness [*im Schoße des Ur-Einen*]. Of course our estheticians have nothing to say about this return to the primordial home . . ."

Mahler, however, apparently did. In this, "the most personal thing I have yet created," he embraces all that had given rise to his symphonic worlds since childhood and youth, and releases it just at the threshold of life; whether the transition from this "Song of the Earth" is to eternal recurrence or a state of permanence, he does not speculate. Perhaps Benjamin Britten summed it up best: that final chord, *gänzlich ersterbend*, is printed on the atmosphere.

Appendix: translation

DAS LIED VON DER ERDE
(The Song of the Earth)

Poems by Li-Po, Ch'ien-Ch'i (?), Mong-Kao-Jen, and Wang-Wei; German paraphrase translations by Hans Bethge from *Die chinesische Flöte: Nachdichtungen chinesischer Lyrik* (Leipzig, 1907). Mahler's interpolations into the texts are underlined.

1 Das Trinklied vom Jammer der Erde (Li-Po)
The Drinking Song of the Misery of the Earth

Schon winkt der Wein im   gold'nen Pokale,
Now   winks the wine in the golden   goblet,

doch trinkt noch nicht, erst sing' ich euch   ein Lied!
but   drink not yet, first sing I to you a song!

Das Lied vom Kummer soll   auf -
The song of   sorrow   should burst -
lachend in die Seele euch   klingen.
laughing in the soul (to) you resound.

Wenn der Kummer naht,   liegen wüst <u>die Gärten der</u>   Seele,
When the sorrow   comes, [then] lie   waste the gardens of the soul,

      <u>Welkt hin und</u> stirbt die Freude, der Gesang.
[Then] dries up and dies the joy,   the singing.

Dunkel ist das   Leben, ist der Tod.
Dark   is (the) life,   is   death.

Herr dieses Hauses!
Lord of this House!

120

Dein Keller birgt die Fülle   des goldenen Weins!
Your cellar holds the abundance of golden   wine!

Hier, diese Laute nenn' ich mein!
Here, this lute call I mine!

Die Laute schlagen und die Gläser   leeren,
The lute   (to) stroke and the glasses (to) empty,

das sind die Dinge die zusammen passen.
those are the things that together   go well.

Ein voller   Becher Weins zur   rechten Zeit
A   brimming cup of wine at the right   time

ist mehr wert, ist mehr wert,
is more worth, is more worth,

ist mehr wert als alle Reiche   dieser Erde!
is more worth than all the kingdoms of this earth!

Dunkel ist das Leben, ist der Tod!
Dark is   life,   is   Death!

Das Firmament blaut   ewig, und die Erde
The heavens   are blue ever, and the earth

wird lange fest steh'n und auf- blüh'n im Lenz.
shall long firm stand and forth- blossom in spring.

Du aber,   Mensch, wie lang lebst denn du?
You, however, man,   how long live then you?

Nicht hundert Jahre darfst du dich   ergötzen,
Not (a) hundred years may   you yourself amuse,

an   all dem morschen Tande dieser Erde!
with all the rotting   trifles of this earth!

Seht dort hinab!   Im   Mondschein auf den Gräbern
See there o'er there! In the moonlight   on the gravestones

hockt   eine wild- gespenstische Gestalt.
crouches a   wildly- ghost-like-eerie Form.

Ein Aff'   ist's! Hört ihr, wie sein Heulen
A   monkey it is! Hear you, how his howling

hinausgellt in den süßen Duft des <u>Lebens</u>!
shrieks forth into the sweet scent of life!

Jetzt nehmt den Wein! Jetzt ist es Zeit, Genossen!
Now take the wine! Now is it time, companions!

Leert eure gold'nen Becher zu Grund!
Empty your golden cups to the bottom!

Dunkel ist das Leben, ist der Tod!
Dark is life, is death!

2 <u>Der</u> Einsame im Herbst (Ch'ien-Ch'i [?])
The Lonely One in Autumn

Herbstnebel wallen bläulich überm <u>See</u>,
Autumn hazes well up bluish o'er the lake,

vom Reif bezogen stehen alle Gräser;
with frost covered stand all the grasses;

man meint, ein Künstler habe Staub von Jade
one would think an artist had a powder of jade

über die feinen <u>Blüten</u> ausgestreut.
over the fine blossoms strewn.

Der süße Duft der Blumen ist verflogen;
The sweet scent of the flowers has vanished;

ein kalter Wind beugt ihre Stengel nieder.
a cold wind bends their stems down.

Bald werden die verwelkten, gold'nen Blätter
Soon will the withered, golden leaves

der Lotosblüten auf dem Wasser zieh'n.
of the lotus blossoms on the water float.

Mein Herz ist müde. Meine kleine Lampe
My heart is tired. My little lamp

erlosch mit Knistern, es gemahnt mich an den Schlaf.
went out with crackling, it calls me to sleep.

122

Ich komm' zu dir, traute Rühestätte!
I   come to you, beloved resting place!

Ja, gib mir <u>Ruh</u>', ich hab' Erquickung   Not!
Yes, give me rest, I   have (of) refreshment need!

Ich weine viel in meinen Einsamkeiten.
I   weep much in my   lonelinesses.

Der Herbst in meinem Herzen währt zu lange.
The autumn in my   heart   lasts too long.

Sonne der Liebe, willst du nie   mehr scheinen,
Sun   of love,   will you never more shine

um   meine bittern Tränen <u>mild</u> aufzutrocknen?
in order my   bitter tears   mildly to dry up?

3 <u>Von der Jugend</u> [Bethge: Der Pavillon aus Porzellan] (Li-Po)
   Of Youth [Bethge: The Pavilion Made of Porcelain]

Mitten in dem kleinen Teiche
Midway in the little   pond

steht   ein Pavillon aus grünem
stands a   pavilion of green

und aus weißem Porzellan.
and of white   porcelain.

Wie der Rücken eines Tigers
Like the back   of a tiger

wölbt die Brücke sich aus Jade
arches the bridge (itself) of jade

zu dem Pavillon hinüber.
to the pavilion (across).

In dem Häuschen sitzen Freunde,
In the cottage   sit   friends,

schön   gekleidet, trinken, plaudern,
beautifully dressed,   drinking, chatting,

123

manche schreiben Verse nieder.
several writing   verses down.

Ihre   seidnen Ärmel gleiten
Their silken   sleeves slide

rückwärts, ihre seidnen Mützen
backwards, their silken   caps

hocken lustig tief   im   Nacken.
crouch drolly deep on the nape of the neck.

Auf des kleinen Teiches stiller
On the small   pond's still

Wasserfläche zeigt sich   alles
water surface shows (itself) everything

wunderlich im Spiegelbilde.
curiously   in mirror image.

Alles   auf dem Kopfe stehend
Everything on its   head   standing

in dem Pavillon aus grünem
in the   pavilion of   green

und aus weißem Porzellan;
and of   white   porcelain;

wie ein Halbmond scheint die Brücke,
like a   halfmoon   seems the bridge,

umgekehrt   der Bogen. Freunde,
upside-down the arch.   Friends,

schön   gekleidet, trinken, plaudern.
beautifully dressed,   drinking, chatting.

124

4 Von der Schönheit [Bethge: Am Ufer] (Li-Po)
Of Beauty [Bethge: On the Bank]

Junge Mädchen   pflücken Blumen,
Young maidens are picking flowers,

pflücken Lotosblumen an dem Uferrande.
picking lotus blossoms on the shore's edge.

Zwischen Büschen und Blättern sitzen sie,
Midst   bushes   and leaves   sit   they,

sammeln Blüten   in den Schoß und rufen
collecting blossoms in their laps   and call

sich einander   Neckereien   zu.
to   each other teasing banter (to).

Gold'ne Sonne   webt   um   die Gestalten,
Golden sunlight weaves around the figures,

spiegelt sie   im   blanken Wasser wider.
mirrors them in the smooth water   (against).

Sonne   spiegelt ihre schlanken Glieder,
Sunlight mirrors their slender   limbs,

ihre süßen Augen wider,
their sweet eyes   (against [i. e., against the water]),

und der Zephir hebt mit Schmeichelkosen
and the zephyr lifts with coaxing caresses

das Gewebe ihrer   Ärmel auf,
the fabric   of their sleeves up,

führt den Zauber ihrer   Wohlgerüche durch   die Luft.
wafts the magic of their lovely scent   through the air.

O sieh, was tummeln sich für schöne   Knaben
O see, how romp about   the handsome lads

dort an dem Uferrand   auf mut'gen Rossen,
there on the shore's edge on spirited horses,

weithin   glänzend wie die Sonnenstrahlen;
into the distance gleaming like the sun's rays;

schon zwischen dem Geäst   der   grünen Weiden
now   amidst   the   branches of the green   willows

trabt das jungfrische   Volk einher!
trots the young-vigorous band over here!

Das Roß   des einen wiehert fröhlich auf,
The horse of one   neighs joyfully forth,

und scheut, und saust   dahin,
and shies,   and rushes off,

über Blumen,   Gräser wanken hin die Hufe,
o'er flowers [and] grasses stagger back the hoofs,

sie   zerstampfen jäh im Sturm die hingesunk'nen Blüten,
they trample   fast in tumult the downfallen   blossoms,

hei! wie flattern im Taumel seine Mähnen,
ho! how flutters in frenzy his   mane,

dampfen   heiß die Nüstern!
[and] steam hot the nostrils!

Gold'ne Sonne webt um   die Gestalten,
Golden sunlight weaves around the figures,

spiegelt sie   im   blanken Wasser wider.
mirrors them in the smooth water (against).

Und die schönste von den Jungfrau'n sendet
And the fairest of the maidens   sends

lange Blicke ihm   der Sehnsucht nach.
long glances to him of longing   (after).

Ihre stolze Haltung ist nur Verstellung.
Her proud bearing is only pretence.

In dem Funkeln ihrer großen Augen,
In the sparkling of her large eyes,

in dem Dunkel ihres heißen Blicks
in the darkness of her hot   glance

126

schwingt klagend noch die Erregung ihres Herzens nach.
reverberates plaintively still the agitation of her heart within.

5 Der Trunkene im Frühling [Bethge: Der Trinker im Frühling] (Li-Po)
The Drunk in Springtime [Bethge: The Drinker in Springtime]

Wenn nur ein Traum das Leben ist,
Since only a dream (the) life is,

warum denn Müh' und Plag'!?
why then toil and torment!?

Ich trinke, bis ich nicht mehr kann,
I drink, 'til I no more can,

den ganzen lieben Tag!
the whole livelong day!

Und wenn ich nicht mehr trinken kann,
And when I no more drinking can,

weil Kehl' und Seele voll,
because throat and soul [are] full,

so tauml' ich bis zu meiner Tür
then stagger I up to my door

und schlafe wundervoll!
and sleep wonderfully!

Was hör' ich beim Erwachen? Horch!
What hear I upon awakening? Listen!

Ein Vogel singt im Baum.
A bird sings in the tree.

Ich frag' ihn, ob schon Frühling sei.
I ask him if already spring's come.

Mir ist, als wie im Traum.
For me it's as though in a dream.

Der Vogel zwitschert: Ja! Ja! Der Lenz,
The bird   twitters: Yes! Yes! Spring,

der Lenz ist da,   sei kommen über Nacht!
spring   is here, it's come   over night!

Aus tiefstem Schauen lauscht' ich auf,
In   deepest gazing   listened I   up at him,

der Vogel singt und lacht!   und lacht!
the bird   sings and laughs! and laughs!

Ich fülle mir   den Becher neu
I   fill   myself the cup   anew

und leer'   ihn bis zum Grund
and empty it   to the   bottom

und singe, bis der Mond erglänzt
and sing   'til the moon glows forth

am   schwarzen Firmament!
in the dark   heavens!

Und wenn ich nicht mehr singen kann,
And when I   no   more singing can,

so   schlaf' ich wieder ein.
then to sleep I   again   go.

Was geht   mich denn der Frühling an!?
What matters to me then the spring!?

Laßt mich betrunken sein!
Let   me   drunk   be!

6 Der Abschied
The Farewell

[Bethge: In Erwartung des Freunds] (Mong-Kao-Jen)
[Bethge: In Expectation of the Friend]

Die Sonne scheidet hinter dem Gebirge.
The sun   departs behind the   mountain.

In   alle Täler steigt der Abend   nieder
Into all valleys steps the evening down

mit seinen Schatten, die voll Kühlung   sind.
with its   shadows that full [of] coolness are.

O sieh! wie eine Silberbarke schwebt
O see! like a   silver ship soars

der Mond _am_   _blauen_ _Himmelssee_ herauf.
the moon upon the blue   heavenly lake upward.

Ich spüre eines feinen Windes Weh'n
I   sense a   gentle wind's drift

hinter den dunklen Fichten!
behind the dark   pine trees!

Der Bach singt voller Wohllaut   durch   das Dunkel.
The brook sings full of pleasant melody through the darkness.

Die _Blumen_ _blassen_ im   _Dämmerschein._
The flowers   pale   in the twilight.

Die _Erde_ _atmet_   _voll_ _von_ _Ruh'_ _und_ _Schlaf._
The earth breathes full of   rest and sleep.

Alle _Sehnsucht_ _will_ _nun_ _träumen_,
All longing   will now dream,

die _müden_ Menschen geh'n heimwärts,
the tired   men   go   homewards,

_um_ _im_ _Schlaf_ vergess'nes Glück
so in sleep forgotten happiness

und Jugend   _neu_ zu _lernen!_
and youthfulness anew to learn!

Die Vögel hocken _still_   in _ihren_ Zweigen.
The birds crouch quietly on their branches.

Die Welt schläft   ein!
The world [goes to] sleep!

_Es_ _wehet_ _kühl_ im   _Schatten_ _meiner_ _Fichten._
It breezes cool in the shadow of my   pine trees.

Ich stehe hier und harre   meines Freundes.
I   stand here and wait for my   friend.

Ich harre sein zum letzten Lebewohl.
I   await his last   farewell.

Ich sehne mich,   O Freund, an deiner Seite
I   long (myself), O friend, at your   side

die Schönheit dieses Abends zu genießen.
the beauty   of this evening to enjoy.

Wo   bleibst du? du läßt mich lang allein!
Where are   you? you leave me   long alone!

Ich wandle auf und nieder mit meiner Laute
I   wander up and down with my   lute

auf Wegen, die von weichem Grase schwellen.
on paths   that with soft   grass swell.

O Schönheit, O ewigen   Liebens, Lebens trunk'ne Welt!
O Beauty,   O of eternal love-and-life   drunken world!

[Bethge: Der Abschied des Freundes] (Wang–Wei)
[Bethge: The Farewell of the Friend]

Er stieg   vom   Pferd und reichte ihm den Trunk
He stepped from the horse and offered him the draught

des Abschieds dar.
of farewell   (forth).

Er fragte ihn, wohin er führe
He asked him whither he was going

und auch warum, warum es müßte sein.
and also why,   why it had   to be.

Er sprach, seine Stimme war umflort: Du, mein Freund,
He spoke, his   voice   was veiled: You, my Friend,

mir   war auf dieser Welt   das   Glück   nicht hold!
for me was in this   world (the) Fortune not   favorable!

Wohin ich geh'? Ich geh', ich wandre in die Berge.
Whither I go?   I   go,   I wander to the mountains.

Ich suche Ruhe, Ruhe für mein einsam Herz!
I seek rest, rest for my lonely heart!

Ich wandle nach der Heimat, meiner Stätte!
I wander to the homeland, to my abode!

Ich werde niemals in die Ferne schweifen.
I will nevermore afar roam.

Still ist mein Herz und harret seiner Stunde!
Still is my heart, and awaits its hour!

Die liebe Erde allüberall
The beloved earth all over everywhere

blüht auf im Lenz und grünt aufs neu!
blossoms forth in Spring and greens up anew!

allüberall und ewig blauen licht die Fernen,
everywhere and ever blue brightly the horizons,

Ewig... ewig...
Eternally... ever...

Notes

1 Background: Mahler's "symphonic worlds" before 1908

1 See Alma Mahler's note to *GMB2*, no. 114 (*GMBE*, no. 105, p. 412). Arthur Schopenhauer, *The World as Will and Representation*, 2 vols., trans. E. F. J. Payne (New York, 1966); Richard Wagner, "Beethoven," in *Richard Wagner's Prose Works*, trans. William Ashton Ellis, V: 57–126 (London, 1896; repr. New York, 1966). The pioneering study of these writers' influence on Mahler and his circle is William J. McGrath, *Dionysian Art and Populist Politics in Austria* (New Haven, 1974), esp. chaps. 1–5; for further discussion and references see Stephen E. Hefling, "Mahler: Symphonies 1–4," in *The Nineteenth-Century Symphony*, ed. D. Kern Holoman (New York, 1997), 369–416.

2 Schopenhauer, *World*, I: 110.

3 Ibid., 196, 274–326; see also p. 14 below.

4 Ibid., 275–76; cf. also 330–31.

5 Ibid., 378–412, esp. 404, and 179, 184–85, 195–98.

6 Ibid., 257, 263.

7 Friedrich Nietzsche, *The Birth of Tragedy*, trans. Walter Kaufmann (New York, 1967), 104.

8 Ibid., 125.

9 Ibid., 104–05.

10 Siegfried Lipiner, *Über die Elemente einer Erneuerung religiöser Ideen in der Gegenwart* (Vienna, 1878), 11–12.

11 Siegfried Lipiner, "Einleitung: Zur Erklärung der 'Todtenfeier,'" in *Poetische Werke von Adam Mickiewicz*, trans. Lipiner, vol. II: *Todtenfeier (Dziady)* (Leipzig, 1887), xvi.

12 *NBL2*, 164 (*NBLE*, 154).

13 *GMB2*, no. 167 (*GMBE*, no. 158), 26 March 1896. Further on this topic see Hefling, "Mahler: Symphonies 1–4."

14 See Stephen E. Hefling, "Mahler's 'Todtenfeier' and the Problem of Program Music," *19th Century Music* 12 (1988): 43–44, and Constantin

Floros, *Gustav Mahler*, vol. I: *Die geistige Welt Gustav Mahlers in systematischer Darstellung* (Wiesbaden, 1977), 24 ff.

15 See especially Mahler's letter to Bruno Walter from the summer of 1904: *GMB2*, no. 334 (*GMBE*, no. 313).

16 Bruno Walter, *Gustav Mahler* (Vienna, 1936), trans. James Galston (New York, 1941; repr. 1973), Eng. trans., 105.

17 See e.g. Stuart Feder, "Before Alma . . . Gustav Mahler and 'Das Ewig-Weibliche,'" in *Mahler Studies*, ed. Stephen E. Hefling (Cambridge, 1997), 89–90.

18 *NBL2*, 174–75 (cf. *NBLE*, 240). Mahler had given essentially the same account to Richard Strauss in 1894; see *Gustav Mahler – Richard Strauss: Correspondence 1888–1911*, ed. Herta Blaukopf, trans. Edmund Jephcott (Chicago, 1984), 37.

19 *NBL2*, 50 (*NBLE*, 53).

20 See Hefling, "Mahler's 'Todtenfeier.'"

21 Lipiner, "Einleitung," xix.

22 Walter, *Mahler* (Vienna, 1936), 90–91, Eng. trans., 129. A "syzygy" is a point of conjunction or opposition, as in the dynamics of planetary motion, and is used more generally to identify a couple or pair of opposites.

23 *NBL2*, 62–63 (*NBLE*, 69); cf. also *HLG* 1, 10.

24 See, e.g., *NBL2*, 138 (*NBLE*, 131), June-July, 1899.

25 Alma Mahler, *Gustav Mahler: Memories and Letters*, 4th edn., rev. and enl. Donald Mitchell and Knud Martner, trans. Basil Creighton (London, 1990) [hereinafter *AMML4*], 7.

26 Feder, "Before Alma . . . ," 84–85.

27 *HLGF* I: 305.

28 *NBL2*, 69 (Norman Lebrecht, *Mahler Remembered* [New York, 1988], 7–8); see also Stuart Feder, "Mahler, Dying," *Chord and Discord* 3/2 (1998): 88.

29 *NBL2*, 176 (*NBLE*, 161).

30 *GMB2*, no. 107 (*GMBE*, no. 99), 28 November 1891.

31 *GMB2*, no. 108 (*GMBE*, no. 100), late autumn 1891 or winter of 1891/92.

32 *NBL2*, 184 (not in *NBLE*), 20 March – 6 April 1901.

33 Further on this, see Hefling, "Mahler: Symphonies 1–4," 386; and Hefling, "Techniques of Irony in Mahler's Œuvre," *Actes du Colloque Gustav Mahler Montpellier 1996*, ed. Henry-Louis de La Grange and André Castagné (Castelnau-le-Lez, forthcoming). The incorrect double negative is directly translated from the German.

34 *Thus Spoke Zarathustra*, pt. 1, "On the Three Metamorphoses," trans. Walter Kaufmann, in *The Portable Nietzsche* (New York, 1968), 139.

35 *NBL2*, 198 (*NBLE*, 178).

36 Gustav Theodor Fechner, *Das Büchlein vom Leben nach dem Tode* (1836; repr. with a preface by Wilhelm Wandt, Leipzig, n.d.), trans. Mary C. Wadsworth as *Life After Death* (New York, 1943); cf. Mahler's commentary on the Second Symphony in *NBL2*, 40 (*NBLE*, 44). That Mahler read Fechner during his Hamburg years is confirmed by Ferdinand Pfohl, *Gustav Mahler: Eindrücke und Erinnerungen aus den Hamburger Jahren* [ca. 1924–29], ed. Knud Martner (Hamburg, 1973), 20.

37 Theodor Reik, *The Haunting Melody* (New York, 1953), chap. 18.

38 *NBL2*, p. 138 (*NBLE*, p. 131), June–July, 1899.

39 See the recollections from Bauer-Lechner's manuscript included in Lebrecht, *Mahler Remembered*, 9–10, as well as the selections by Theodor Fischer and Guido Adler (ibid., 19–22).

40 See Robert Bailey, "The Structure of the *Ring* and Its Evolution," *19th Century Music* 1 (1977): 51–52.

41 Further on the "Ewigkeit" motive, see Henry-Louis de La Grange, "Music about Music in Mahler: Reminiscences, Allusions, or Quotations," in *Mahler Studies*, ed. Hefling, 143–44 and 167–68.

42 Theodor W. Adorno, *Mahler: A Musical Physiognomy*, trans. Edmund Jephcott (Chicago, 1992), 77, 78, and 79.

43 Peter Franklin, *Mahler: Symphony No. 3* (Cambridge, 1991).

44 Fechner, *Life after Death*, 89.

45 *Zarathustra*, pt. 3, "The Convalescent," sec. 2, trans. Kaufmann, 333. Earlier, in *Die fröhliche Wissenschaft*, Nietzsche had characterized eternal recurrence as "the eternal hourglass of existence . . . turned upside down again and again, and you with it, speck of dust!" (book 4, §341; trans. Walter Kaufmann as *The Gay Science* [New York, 1974], 273).

46 *NBL2*, 57.

47 *NBL2*, 61 and 68 (*NBLE*, 64 and 67), 4 July and early August 1896.

48 *GMB2*, no. 181 (*GMBE*, no. 169), 1 July 1896.

49 Alfred Roller, *Die Bildnisse von Gustav Mahler* (Leipzig, 1922), 26 (also trans. in Lebrecht, *Mahler Remembered*, 164).

50 *NBL2*, 59 (*NBLE*, 62), 4 July 1896.

51 *NBL2*, 56 (*NBLE*, 58), 22 June 1896.

52 *GMB2*, no. 182 (*GMBE*, no. 170), 2 July 1896.

53 *NBL2*, 59 (*NBLE*, 61–62), 4 July 1896; cf. also the passage entitled "Martyrium" ("Martyrdom") in *NBL2*, 50–51 (*NBLE*, 54), Easter of 1896.

54 Feder, "Mahler, Dying" (1998), 91.

55 *NBL2*, 76 (*NBLE*, 76), October 1896.

56 *NBL2*, 73–74 (*NBLE*, 73), September–October 1896.

57 *NBL2*, 50 and 80; see also 81 (*NBLE*, 54 and 81; see also 83), 2–6 April 1896

and May 1897. Bruno Walter writes similarly in his *Theme and Variations: An Autobiography*, trans. James A. Galston (New York, 1946), 85.

58 Kay R. Jamison, *Touched with Fire: Manic-Depressive Illness and the Artistic Temperament* (New York, 1993), 234 and 338, n. 156, and personal communication from Dr. Stuart Feder, New York; see also American Psychiatric Association, *Diagnostic and Statistical Manual of Mental Disorders*, 4th edn. (Washington, D.C., 1994), 363–65 *et passim*.

59 *NBL2*, 161 and 50 (*NBLE*, 54 and 150).

60 *NBL2*, 179 (*NBLE*, 162), late December 1900. See also *Bruno Walter: Briefe*, 1894–1962, ed. Lotte Walter Lindt (Frankfurt am Main, 1969), 52, and *Gustav Mahler und Holland: Briefe*, ed. Eduard Reeser (Vienna, 1980), 105. Freund Hain (sometimes spelled "Hein") was also the inspiration for Schubert's famous song "Der Tod und das Mädchen [Death and the Maiden]," which later became the centerpiece of his String Quartet in D minor, D. 810.

61 Adorno, *Mahler: A Musical Physiognomy*, 55 and 53.

62 Ibid., 55.

63 Ibid., 96.

64 *NBL2*, 163 (*NBLE*, 152–53); on Strauss's reaction, see *NBL2*, 203 (*NBLE*, 184).

65 Walter, *Briefe*, 52. Cf. also Alma Mahler, *Mein Leben* (Frankfurt am Main, 1960), 32.

66 *GMB2*, preface to the first edition of Mahler's letters by Alma Mahler, xiv–xv (*GMBE*, 25–26). See also *HLG* 1: 16

67 *HLG* 1: 15.

68 See Raymond Joly, "Gustav Mahler: Psychoanalytische Anmerkungen," in *Musik-Konzepte: Sonderband Gustav Mahler*, ed. Heinz-Klaus Metzger and Rainer Riehn (Munich, 1989), 200, and Stuart Feder, "Gustav Mahler, Dying," *International Review of Psycho-Analysis* 5 (1978): 145.

69 *GMB2*, xv (*GMBE*, 26).

70 Bauer-Lechner, "Mahleriana," quoted in *HLG* 2: 334–35 (*HLGF* II: 66–67); de La Grange provides a full account of Mahler's illness and recovery.

71 *NBL2*, 185–86 (not in *NBLE*); see also *HLG* 2: 340 (*HLGF* II: 72–73).

72 See Feder, "Gustav Mahler, Dying" (1978), esp. 130–33; and Feder, "Gustav Mahler um Mitternacht," *International Review of Psycho-Analysis* 7 (1980): 11–26, esp. 18.

73 For further information see also Stephen E. Hefling, "The Rückert Lieder," in *The Mahler Companion*, ed. Donald Mitchell and Andrew Nicholson (Oxford, 1999), chap. 13.

74 *AMML4*, 226.

75 *NBL2*, 194 (*NBLE*, 174), August 1901.

76 *NBL2*, 27 (*NBLE*, 32).

77 Hans and Rosaleen Moldenhauer, *Anton von Webern: A Chronicle of His Life and Work* (New York, 1979), 75. Here, it may be noted, are the roots of Schoenberg's now well-known concepts of *Grundgestalt* and "developing variation"; see his *Style and Idea: Selected Writings of Arnold Schoenberg*, ed. Leonard Stein, trans. Leo Black (Berkeley, 1984), e.g., 91, 397, *et passim*; cf. also Adorno, *Mahler*, 150–51.

78 Cf. *SSLD*, 57–68, and *HLG* 2: 790 ff.

79 *SSLD*, 55.

80 The plan for the Fourth is reproduced, inter alia, in Paul Bekker, *Gustav Mahlers Sinfonien* (Berlin, 1921; repr. Tutzing, 1969), 144–45; a facsimile appears in Edward R. Reilly, "Mahler's Manuscripts and What They Can Tell Us: An Informal Consideration," *Muziek & Wetenschap: Dutch Journal for Musicology* 5/3 (1995–96): 370; cf. also Donald Mitchell, "Eternity or Nothingness? Mahler's Fifth Symphony," in *New Sounds, New Century: Mahler's Fifth and the Royal Concertgebouw Orchestra*, ed. Mitchell (Bussum, 1997), 44 ff.

81 *NBL2*, 193 (*NBLE*, 173), 4 August 1901.

82 *Ein Glück ohne Ruh': Die Briefe Gustav Mahlers an Alma*, ed. Henry-Louis de La Grange and Günther Weiß (Berlin, 1995), no. 107 [14 October 1904] (*AMML4*, 243).

83 Kaufmann, translator's introduction to *The Gay Science*, 7; cf. also 257, n. 54.

84 *Zarathustra*, pt. 1, "On Reading and Writing," and "Zarathustra's Prologue," sec. 5, trans. Kaufmann, 153 and 129.

85 See, e. g., Gilbert E. Kaplan, "From Mahler with Love," in Gustav Mahler, *Adagietto: Facsimile, Documentation, Recording*, ed. Kaplan (New York, 1992), 26 ff.; Constantin Floros, *Gustav Mahler: The Symphonies*, trans. Vernon Wicker (Portland, Oreg., 1993), 154–55; and Mitchell, "Eternity or Nothingness?," 49–51.

86 Reinhard Gerlach, *Strophen von Leben, Traum und Tod: Ein Essay über Rückert-Lieder von Gustav Mahler*, Taschenbücher zur Musikwissenschaft, ed. Richard Schaal, no. 83 (Wilhelmshaven, 1982), 96 ff., here at 103; cf. also Adorno's famous reading of this finale and the related movement of the Seventh, 136 ff.

87 *Zarathustra*, pt. 4, "The Drunken Song," sec. 10, trans. Kaufmann, 435. Cf. also Floros's reading of the Rondo-Finale in the Seventh as a reflection of eternal recurrence (*Gustav Mahler: The Symphonies*, 211).

88 Trans. Kaufmann, 340 ff. Cf. also Floros, *Gustav Mahler: The Symphonies*, 211.

89 *HLG* 2: 825.
90 See the program listing of the Viennese premiere in Knud Martner, *Gustav Mahler im Konzertsaal: Eine Dokumentation seiner Konzerttätigkeit* (Copenhagen, 1985), 98, and *AMML4*, 70.
91 On this movement see especially Robert Samuels, *Mahler's Sixth Symphony: A Study in Musical Semiotics* (Cambridge, 1995), 94–132; Floros, *Gustav Mahler*, vol. II: *Mahler und die Symphonik des 19. Jahrhunderts in never Deutung* (Wiesbaden, 1977), 165–78, as well as *Gustav Mahler: The Symphonies*, 176–78; and *AMML4*, 70.
92 See above, p. 2; cf. also Adorno, 97.
93 See Hefling, "Techniques of Irony in Mahler's Œuvre."
94 See Floros, *Gustav Mahler: The Symphonies*, 190 ff., and *AMML4*, 89.
95 For further discussion, see Stephen E. Hefling, "'Ihm in die Lieder zu blicken': Mahler's Seventh Symphony Sketchbook," in *Mahler Studies*, ed. Hefling, 187–88 and 211.
96 Reported by Richard Specht in "Thematische Novitäten-Analysen: I. Mahlers Siebente Symphonie," *Der Merker* 1/2 (1909): 1; see also *HLGF* III: 366 and *HLGF* II: 1205. For a review of literature on the Seventh, see *HLGF* II: 1181–1213; further discussion is found in *The Seventh Symphony of Gustav Mahler: A Symposium*, ed. James L. Zychowicz (Cincinnati and Madison, 1990), Adorno, *Mahler*, esp. 136 ff., and Hefling, "Techniques of Irony."
97 Henry-Louis de La Grange, "L'Enigme de la Septième," in *The Seventh Symphony*, ed. Zychowicz, 24.
98 Conversation with Mahler reported by Richard Specht, *Gustav Mahler* (Berlin, 1913), 304; see also Floros, *Gustav Mahler: The Symphonies*, 214.
99 *GMB2*, no. 360 (*GMBE*, no. 338), August 1906.
100 Moldenhauer, *Anton von Webern*, 135. Mahler presumably meant the passage leading into the recapitulation of the first movement (fig. 55 ff.), although the text in question also appears earlier (fig. 38).
101 Specht, *Mahler*, 304. For further discussion of the Eighth, see esp. *A "Mass" for the Masses: Proceedings of the Mahler VIII Symposium, Amsterdam 1988*, ed. Eveline Nikkels and Robert Becqué (Rijswijk, 1992).

2 Genesis

1 *GMB2*, no. 364 (*GMBE*, no. 341), 12 September 1906; Lebrecht, 208. Further documentation concerning Mahler's departure from the Opera and the other events of 1907 will be found in *HLGF* III, chaps. 49–50.
2 Walter, *Gustav Mahler*, Eng. trans., 52.

3 Alma Mahler, *Gustav Mahler: Erinnerungen und Briefe*, 2nd edn. (Amsterdam, 1949), 151 (not in *AMML4*).

4 *GMB2*, no. 371 (*GMBE*, no. 350), June 1907.

5 *AMML4*, 105. See also *HLGF* III: 83 and 541.

6 *AMML4*, 122. On the family history of heart problems, see *AMML4*, 6–7 (*Erinnerungen und Briefe*, 13–14).

7 In a number of articles and lectures dating from 1969, de La Grange has suggested that Alma Mahler deliberately exaggerated the extent to which Mahler's heart disease affected his last years (see the bibliography in *HLG* 1: 959 [*HLGF* I: 1090]; see also *HLGF* III: 80–90, 99–100, 478–79, 537–41, 754–63, *et passim*, as well as de La Grange, "'Ma musique est vécue': La biographie comme outil d'analyse," *Colloque international Gustav Mahler 25. 26. 27. janvier 1985* (Paris, 1986), 36; "'Meine Musik ist "gelebt"': Mahler's Biography as a Key to His Works," *Opus* 3/2 (February 1987): 16–17; and "Auf der Suche nach Gustav Mahler: Eine Bilanz," in *Gustav Mahler*, ed. Hermann Danuser, Wege der Forschung, vol. 653 (Darmstadt, 1992), 56 ff. Influenced by this view, Vera Micznik and Anthony Newcomb both claim that Mahler's personal circumstances are not relevant to an interpretation of late Mahler, particularly the Ninth Symphony (Micznik, "Is Mahler's Music Autobiographical? A Reappraisal," *Review Mahler Revue* 1 [1987]: 47–63; Micznik, "The Farewell Story of Mahler's Ninth," *19th Century Music* 20 [1996]: 144–66; Newcomb, "Narrative Archetypes and Mahler's Ninth Symphony," in *Music and Text: Critical Inquiries*, ed. Steven Paul Scher [Cambridge, 1992], 118–36, esp. 120).

8 Roller, *Die Bildnisse*, 18–19 (Eng. trans. in Lebrecht, *Mahler Remembered*, 158).

9 Walter, *Briefe*, 95.

10 "under the semblance of death": Walter, *Mahler*, Eng. trans., 123; quotation from 54.

11 Theodor von Jürgensen, *Erkrankungen der Kreislaufsorgane: Klappenfehler*, Specielle Pathologie und Therapie, ed. Hermann Nothnagel, vol. XV, pt. 1, sec. 4 (Vienna, 1903), 46; see also 1–7 and 42–45. Cf. also Jürgensen (in the same series), *Endocarditis*, vol. XV, pt. 1, sec. 3 (Vienna, 1900), 1–25 and 165–77, and *Insufficenz (Schwäche) des Herzens*, vol. XV, pt. 1, sec. 1 (Vienna, 1899), 64 *et passim*. Further on valvulitis and endocarditis, see Fredrick A. Willius and Thomas J. Dry, *A History of the Heart and the Circulation* (Philadelphia, 1948), 135–223; James B. Herrick, *A Short History of Cardiology* (Springfield, Ill., 1942), 176–86; and William Osler's influential Gulstonian Lectures, "Malignant Endocarditis," *British Medical Journal* 1 [1885], 467–70, 522–26, 577–79. On Mahler's medical history see

Nicholas P. Christy, Beverly M. Christy, and Barry G. Wood, "Gustav Mahler and His Illnesses," *Transactions of the American Clinical and Climatological Association* 82 (1970): 200–17; Feder, "Gustav Mahler, Dying" (1978): 125–48; David Levy, "Gustav Mahler and Emanuel Libman: Bacterial Endocarditis in 1911," *British Medical Journal* 293 (1986): 1628–31; Susan M. Filler, "Mahler in the Medical Literature," *News About Mahler Research* 23 (March 1990): 8–13; John O'Shea, *Was Mozart Poisoned? Medical Investigations into the Lives of the Great Composers* (New York, 1991), 180–86; Nicholas P. Christy and Beverly M. Christy, "Mahler's Final Illness," *Chord and Discord* 3/2 (1998): 69–76; Stuart Feder, "The Diagnosis – Terminal but not Final: A Commentary on the Christys' Paper," and "Mahler, Dying," *Chord and Discord* 3/2 (1998): 77–102.

12 See *HLG* 2, 334 ff.; Feder, "Gustav Mahler, Dying" (1978): 146; Christy, Christy, and Wood, "Gustav Mahler and His Illnesses," 212; and *HLGF* III: 959–60.

13 *AMML4*, 123–24. In *And the Bridge is Love* (New York, 1958), 35, Alma further misdates Mahler's receipt of the Bethge volume, claiming it had arrived "several years previously," and that "he had always intended to use these verses sometime . . ." The "old consumptive friend" was Hofrat Dr. Theobald Pollak, a director in the Austrian Railroad Ministry, who later became a modest supporter of Schoenberg and his school; Pollack is mentioned frequently in *Alma Mahler-Werfel: Diaries 1898–1902*, ed. and trans. Antony Beaumont (London, 1998); see also *The Berg–Schoenberg Correspondence: Selected Letters*, ed. Juliane Brand, Christopher Hailey, and Donald Harris, trans. J. Brand and C. Hailey (New York, 1987), 46, 48–49, 53–54, 56.

14 *Börsenblatt für den Deutschen Buchhandel* (Leipzig, 1907), 10130 (I am grateful to Knud Martner for providing me with this citation); *HLGF* III: 94.

15 Roller, *Die Bildnisse*, 18–19 (Eng. trans. in Lebrecht, 158).

16 *AMML4*, 127.

17 See above, p. 17.

18 Letter to Carl Moll of 16 February 1908, published in Zoltan Roman, *Gustav Mahler's American Years: A Documentary History* (Stuyvesant, NY, 1989), 82.

19 *GMB2*, nos. 379, 381, and 383 (*GMBE*, nos. 358, 362, and 363).

20 *GMB2*, no. 390 (*GMBE*, no. 368), 17 April 1908.

21 Letter to Carl Moll, *GMB2*, no. 395 (*GMBE*, no. 373); angina here probably refers to inflammation of the throat (pharyngitis) rather than to the heart condition angina pectoris (see Christy and Christy, "Mahler's Final Illness," 74–75).

22 *GMB2*, no. 394 (*GMBE*, no. 372). "The latest Don Quixote prank" is probably a reference to "the cuts affair": Weingartner, Mahler's successor at the Opera, had reintroduced cuts in performances of Wagner's *Die Walküre*, which Mahler had always performed complete. On 17 June Weingartner's entrance to conduct that opera was greeted by an angry scene punctuated by cries of "Hoch Mahler!" Five people were arrested and polemical exchanges in the newspapers followed.

23 See Walter, *Theme and Variations*, 164–68; Emanuel E. Garcia, "Bruno Walter Consults Sigmund Freud," *Journal of the Conductors' Guild* 11 (1990): 24–31; Ernst von Feuchtersleben, *Hygiene of the Mind*, trans. F. C. Sumner (New York, 1933), esp. chap. 11 and pp. 116–19; cf. also William M. Johnston, *The Austrian Mind: An Intellectual and Social History, 1848–1938* (Berkeley, 1972), 226.

24 *GMB2*, no. 396 (*GMBE*, no. 375).

25 Alma Mahler, *Erinnerungen und Briefe*, 176 (*AMML4*, 140).

26 Walter, *Gustav Mahler*, Eng. trans., 61–62. Mahler also told this story to Alfred Roller, who reported it slightly differently (see Lebrecht, 164). On the dating of this occurrence, see *HLGF* III: 346.

27 *Erinnerungen und Briefe*, 175 (*AMML4*, 139).

28 *GMB2*, no. 400 (*GMBE*, no. 378).

29 Hans Heilmann, *Chinesische Lyrik, vom 12. Jahrhundert v. Chr. bis zur Gegenwart* (Munich, 1905); Le Marquis d'Hervey de Saint-Denys, *Poésies de l'époque des Thang* (Paris, 1862); Judith Gautier, *Le livre de jade: poésies traduites du chinois* (Paris, 1862), 2nd edn. (Paris, 1902). The most important studies of the sources for Bethge's *Nachdichtungen* and Mahler's use of them are *HLGF* III: 1121–64 and Fusako Hamao, "The Sources of the Texts in Mahler's *Das Lied von der Erde*," *19th Century Music* 19 (1995): 83–95. Other useful discussions include *SSLD*, 162–442; Arthur Wenk, "The Composer as Poet in *Das Lied von der Erde*," *19th Century Music* 1 (1977): 33–47; Zoltan Roman, "Mahler's Songs and Their Influence on His Symphonic Thought" (Ph.D. diss., University of Toronto, 1970), 106–23; Kii-Ming Lo, "Chinesische Dichtung als Text-Grundlage für Mahlers 'Lied von der Erde,'" in *Das Gustav-Mahler-Fest Hamburg 1989: Bericht über den Internationalen Gustav-Mahler-Kongreß*, ed. Matthias Theodor Vogt (Kassel, 1991), 509–28; and Stephen E. Hefling, "*Das Lied von der Erde*: Mahler's Symphony for Voices and Orchestra – or Piano," *Journal of Musicology* 10 (1992): 293–341, esp. 316 ff.

30 The original Chinese texts and Bethge's versions are reproduced in *HLGF* III, *SSLD*, and Kii-Ming Lo, "Chinesische Dichtung"; de La Grange also provides the French translations noted above, and Mitchell includes

photofacsimiles of Heilmann's German translations; Lo provides transcriptions of all these sources.

31 Eberhard Bethge, "Hans Bethge and *Das Lied von der Erde*," trans. Morten Solvik, *News about Mahler Research* 35 (April 1996): 18.

32 Hans Bethge, *Die chinesische Flöte: Nachdichtungen chinesischer Lyrik* (Leipzig, 1907), 109. In the present volume the names of the Chinese poets are given in modern form according to the Wade–Giles romanization system; Bethge actually uses the form "Li-Tai-Po." (In the Pinyin system the poet's name is spelled "Li-Bai.")

33 Eberhard Bethge, "Hans Bethge and *Das Lied von der Erde*," 20.

34 Adorno, 148, 149, 150.

35 See *AMML4*, 109.

36 For further information and references on this topic, see e. g., Edward R. Reilly, "An Inventory of Musical Sources," *News about Mahler Research* 2 (Dec. 1977), 3–5; Reilly, "Mahler's Manuscripts and What They Can Tell Us"; Hefling, "*Das Lied von der Erde*: Mahler's Symphony for Voices and Orchestra – or Piano," and Hefling, "The Composition of 'Ich bin der Welt abhanden gekommen,'" in *Gustav Mahler*, ed. Hermann Danuser, 96–158.

37 *NBL2*, 117 (*NBLE*, 116).

38 *GMB2*, no. 429 (*GMBE*, no. 407).

39 A case in point is his performance of the *Kindertotenlieder* with Johannes Messchaert in 1907; see *Gustav Mahler und Holland*, ed. Reeser, 74–84, and *HLGF* II: 1053–57. It is also noteworthy that Bruno Walter apparently considered giving the first Viennese performance of *Das Lied von der Erde* at the keyboard, as a letter from Alban Berg to Arnold Schoenberg reveals: "I heard privately that the Merker [*Der Merker*, arts periodical published in Vienna] is sponsoring a matinee during the Music Festival [*Wiener Musikfestwoche*, late June 1912]: Rosé will play a Beethoven Quartet – and, of all the tasteless things: Walter will play *Das Lied von der Erde* on the piano with Weidemann and Miller . . ." (dated 5 June 1912; in *Berg–Schoenberg Correspondence*, ed. Brand, Hailey, and Harris, 94; the German text will be found in Hermann Danuser, *Gustav Mahler: Das Lied von der Erde*, Meisterwerke der Musik, vol. XXV (Munich, 1986), 117. This projected performance did not take place, and was not publicly announced in either *Der Merker* or the *Neue freie Presse*; nonetheless, it suggests that Walter (unlike Berg) knew Mahler had originally planned the work for orchestra or piano.

40 Ed. Stephen E. Hefling (Vienna, 1989). Further on this source, see the preface to the edition, as well as Hefling, "*Das Lied von der Erde*: Mahler's Symphony for Voices and Orchestra – or Piano."

41 Archives of Universal Edition, Vienna; photocopy at the Internationale Gustav Mahler Gesellschaft, Vienna.

42 Letter of 26 November 1909 to Emil Hertzka, director of Universal Edition; see Hans Moldenhauer, "Unbekannte Briefe Gustav Mahlers an Emil Hertzka," *Neue Zeitschrift für Musik* 135 (1974): 544.

43 Stein's edition is copyrighted 1942, Universal Edition / Hawkes & Son Ltd. (London), plate number 3391. His book *Orpheus in New Guises* (London, 1953), opp. p. 7, includes a facsimile of the last page from the fourth movement of Mahler's piano autograph (also reproduced in Danuser, *Das Lied von der Erde*, facsimile IV).

44 For a complete listing and discussion, see Hefling, "*Das Lied von der Erde*: Mahler's Symphony for Voices and Orchestra – or Piano," esp. 311–13, 321–22, 326, and 339–40.

45 Vienna, Stadt- und Landesbibliothek; see also *HLGF* III: 1123.

46 Walter, *Theme and Variations*, 193.

47 Korngold, "Feuilleton: Neue Musik," *Neue freie Presse*, morning edn., 9 November 1912, pp. 2 and 3; *Berg–Schoenberg Correspondence*, ed. Brand, Hailey, and Harris, 125.

48 Letter to Wolfgang Stresemann, Intendant of the Berlin Philharmonic, 5 December 1957, in Walter, *Briefe*, 355.

49 *Conversations with Klemperer*, comp. and ed. Peter Heyworth (London: Victor Gollancz Ltd., 1973), 33.

3 Reception

1 For a more complete overview, see *HLGF* III: 1063–68; statistics on performances of Mahler's works through 1914 compiled by Guido Adler will be found in Edward R. Reilly, *Gustav Mahler and Guido Adler: Records of a Friendship* (Cambridge, 1982), 71–72.

2 See *HLGF* III: 807–32.

3 See *Gustav Mahler Dokumentation: Sammlung Eleonore Vondenhoff*, comp. Bruno and Eleanore Vondenhoff, 2 vols. (Tutzing, 1978–83), I: 406–09, II: 203–04.

4 William Ritter, "Une nouvelle symphonie de Mahler," *La Vie Musicale* 5/7 (1 December 1911), 136 and 138.

5 *AMML4*, 187 and 143.

6 See above, p. 18.

7 Ritter, "Une nouvelle symphonie," 139.

8 Walter, *Gustav Mahler*, 46 (Eng. trans., 59).

9 Walter, *Theme and Variations*, 187–88. The premiere of the Eighth Sym-

phony took place on 12–13 September 1910, and Mahler left Vienna on 16 October en route to New York for what would be his final season there (see *HLGF* III: 833–40).

10 Ritter, "Une nouvelle symphonie," 140.

11 Further on Mahler and Specht, see Herta Blaukopf, "Amsterdam 1920: Sechs Zeitzeugen feiern Mahler," *Muziek & Wetenschap: Dutch Journal for Musicology* 5 (1995–96): 356–58.

12 A footnote signed G.[eorges] H.[umbert] on p. 136 of Ritter's article "Une nouvelle symphonie" indicates that the designation "Lied-Symphonie" came from Gutmann's press release. Humbert was chief editor of the publication (*HLGF* III: 394, n. 108).

13 See *HLGF* III: 772–79, 848–50, 1074–75, *et passim*. Alma refused Gropius's proposal that they live together during the summer of 1911, and did not marry him until 1915, after her stormy affair with Kokoschka.

14 William Ritter, "Le chant de la terre, de Gustave Mahler," *Gazette de Lausanne*, no. 326 (26 November 1911), [2].

15 See Peter Heyworth, *Otto Klemperer: His Life and Times*, 2 vols. (Cambridge, 1983), I: 62–63 and 66–68; Alma Mahler, *Mein Leben*, 52–53 and 56–62; and *Berg–Schoenberg Correspondence*, ed. Brand, Hailey, and Harris, 85–87.

16 Otto Klemperer, *Gustav Mahler: Erinnerungen und Briefe* (Vienna, 1949), trans. Basil Creighton as *Gustav Mahler: Memories and Letters* (London, 1968); reprinted in *Klemperer on Music: Shavings from a Musician's Workbench*, ed. Martin Anderson (London, 1986), 155.

17 Schoenberg, *Style and Idea*, 447 ff.

18 See Stephen E. Hefling, "Gustav Mahler and Arnold Schönberg," in *Mahler's Unknown Letters*, ed. Herta Blaukopf (London, 1986), 167–76.

19 German text printed in Danuser, *Das Lied von der Erde*, 114–15. Here and in the following letter to Berg, Webern's phrase "to give up the ghost [*den Geist aufgeben*]" may be an allusion to the Gospel accounts of Jesus' giving up his spirit on the cross.

20 Moldenhauer, *Anton von Webern*, 150–51.

21 "Soul" (*Seele*), which Webern emphasizes here, was one of Mahler's textual interpolations; Bethge's version reads "Weil Leib und Kehle voll [Because belly and throat are full]." Some of the lines Webern cites differ slightly from Mahler's, probably because he is quoting from memory.

22 Rudolf Louis, *Die deutsche Musik der Gegenwart*, 2nd edn. (Munich, 1909), 182; cf. also *HLG* 2: 305, n. 82, as well as Louis's reviews of the Seventh Symphony cited in *HLGF* III: 384–85.

23 See *HLG* 2: 660–64 and *HLGF* III: 349 and 735–36.

24 "O Schönheit, o ewigen Liebens, Lebens trunk'ne Welt [O Beauty! O world drunken of eternal love-and-life!]" is Mahler's own interpolation into the text at the climax to the first part of "Der Abschied" (fig. 34–4 ff.).
25 German text reproduced in part in Danuser, *Das Lied von der Erde*, 111.
26 See *HLG* 2: 395 ff. *et passim*; Mahler's letters to Ritter, ed. Bruno and Eleonore Vondenhoff, are published in *Mahler's Unknown Letters*, ed. Blaukopf, 139–49.
27 See Allan Janik and Stephen Toulmin, *Wittgenstein's Vienna* (New York, 1973), 45–46.
28 See Lebrecht, 182.
29 See above, p. 17.
30 In *Gustav Mahler* (1913), 346, Specht has changed "erotisches Menuett" to "exotisches Menuet."
31 See chap. 4 below, esp. 116–19. Specht must have been quoting from memory: Wagner's text actually reads "wehendem All [billowing All]."
32 German text partially reprinted in Danuser, *Das Lied von der Erde*, 111–12.

4 The music

1 See above, p. 72.
2 Johnston, *The Austrian Mind*, 174.
3 See his letter to Alma of June 1909 concerning the conclusion of *Faust* and the Eternal Feminine in *Ein Glück ohne Ruh'*, ed. de La Grange and Weiß, no. 276 (*AMML4*, 319–21, esp. 321).
4 Cf. also *SSLD*, 370–73 and 424–31.
5 See Johnston, *The Austrian Mind*, chap. 11, "Fascination with Death."
6 Robert Bailey, "*Das Lied von der Erde*: Tonal Language and Formal Design," unpublished paper presented to the Forty-Fourth Annual Meeting of the American Musicological Society, Minneapolis, October 1978, and also to the Colorado MahlerFest, Boulder, January 1998. Figures 1, 2, and 4 in this handbook are modified versions of Bailey's analytical diagrams, which were published with his kind permission in Hefling, "*Das Lied von der Erde*: Mahler's Symphony for Voices and Orchestra – or Piano," and are reproduced here by permission of *The Journal of Musicology*.
7 *NBL2*, 158 (*NBLE*, 147), 13 July 1900. Further on the revisions of the first movement, see Hefling, "*Das Lied von der Erde*: Mahler's Symphony for Voices and Orchestra – or Piano," 303–11.
8 Reilly, *Gustav Mahler and Guido Adler*, 66–68, at 68.
9 Precisely what Mahler knew about pentatonicism remains uncertain. He probably heard native East Asian music when he visited the Paris Exhibi-

tion of 1900 while on tour with the Vienna Philharmonic (see *HLG* 2: 255–57 [*HLGF* I: 879]; for examples of the various musics performed there, see Judith Gautier, *Les musiques bizarres à l'Exposition de 1900* [Paris, 1900]). During his last years Mahler admired Debussy's music (which makes substantial use of pentatonicism) and performed several of Debussy's orchestral works with the New York Philharmonic, although we do not know when he first became familiar with them; he was, however, planning to add *Pelléas et Mélisande* to the Hofoper repertoire as early as November 1906, a project he was unable to carry out (see *HLGF* II: 953 and III: 1003 *et passim*). There is anecdotal evidence that Mahler may have heard cylinder recordings of Chinese music near the time he was composing *Das Lied von der Erde* (see *HLGF* III: 341 and 1128). Various studies of pentatonicism had been published at the time, including a lengthy article in Hermann Mendel's *Musikalisches Conversations-Lexikon* (Berlin, 1870–79), s.v. "China," by C. Billert (including a discussion of heptatonic scales, p. 405); Antoine Dechevrens, "Etude sur le système musical chinois," *Sammelbände der Internationalen Musikgesellschaft* 2 (1900–01): esp. 526–47 (with numerous musical examples); and Otto Abraham and Erich M. von Hornbostel, "Studien über das Tonsystem und die Musik der Japaner," *Sammelbände der Internationalen Musikgesellschaft* 4 (1902–3): 302–60, which includes discussion of the "Japanese" (hemitonic) pentatonic scale form *Hirajoshi*. See also Tran van Khe, "Le pentatonique, est-il universel? Quelques réflexions sur le pentatonisme," *The World of Music* 19/1–2 (1977): 85–91.

10 See above, pp. 20–21.

11 Other notable instances occur at figs. 1+3 ff., 3–4, 15+5 through 16+2, and 36 through 37+2.

12 Adorno, *Mahler*, 150, and *SSLD*, 62, 125–27, 393, and 406. See also *SSLD*'s Appendix C, 624–31, an English translation of Guido Adler's 1908 article "Über Heterophonie"; perhaps Adler gave Mahler information on the topic, which had also been discussed in the articles by Dechevrens and by Hornbostel and Abraham cited in n. 9 above. But Reinhold Brinkmann has pointed out ("Das ungenaue Unisono: Sechs Kommentare zu Schumanns 'Zwielicht,'" *Musik-Konzepte*, vol. XCV: *Schumann und Eichendorff*, ed. Heinz-Klaus Metzger and Rainer Riehn [Munich, 1997], 60 ff.) that there was a Romantic European tradition of the imprecise unison extending back to Schumann's "Zwielicht [Twilight]" (no. 10 in the Eichendorff *Liederkreis*, Op. 39), where the technique occurs in an affective context of alienation and loss of identity. (I am grateful to Prof. Brinkmann for bringing this to my attention.)

13 Adorno, *Mahler*, 149–50. The Dolomites are a range of southeastern Alps

in the South Tyrol near Toblach, where Mahler composed *Das Lied* and the Ninth and Tenth Symphonies.

14 See above, p. 60.

15 See Allen Forte, *The Structure of Atonal Music* (New Haven, 1973).

16 The refrain also bears a striking resemblance to the head-motive of Schumann's *Etudes symphoniques* for piano, Op. 13. The chain of possible associations is complex. In brief, it was generally known in Mahler's day that Schumann took this theme, which he described as "grave," "pathetic," and a "quasi marche funebre," from the father of Ernestine von Fricken, the seventeen-year-old girl with whom he was in love at the time (1834); Schumann subsequently broke with her upon learning that she was born out of wedlock. The finale of the *Etudes* quotes a theme from Marschner's opera *Der Templer und die Jüdin* (*The Knight Templar and the Jewess*, based on Sir Walter Scott's *Ivanhoe*), which, as its title suggests, explores the problem of a protagonist psychologically divided within himself (Mahler had conducted it in 1886). Moreover, the Marschner quotation contains the words "you proud Englishman, rejoice," which Schumann intended as a homage to his friend, the composer Sterndale Bennett. Mahler's allusion to the Symphonic Etudes may thus be a bittersweet return of compliments to Schumann, whom he deeply admired. (See Wilhelm Joseph von Wasielewski, *Life of Robert Schumann*, trans. A. L. Alger [Boston, 1871, repr. Detroit, 1975], 87–89 and 201–2; Wasielewski, *Robert Schumann: Eine Biographie*, 4th edn. [Leipzig, 1906, repr. Walluf bei Wiesbaden, 1972], 138–45 and 150–52; J. A. Fuller-Maitland, *Schumann* [New York, 1884], 21–22 and 53–54; *HLGF* I: 239; *Early Letters of Robert Schumann*, ed. Clara Schumann, trans. May Herbert [London, 1888, repr. St. Clair Shores, Mich., 1970], 239–40; and, on the general problem of quotation in Mahler, de La Grange, "Music about Music in Mahler: Reminiscences, Allusions, or Quotations?")

17 Walter, *Gustav Mahler*, Eng. trans., 34–35.

18 Cf. also *SSLD*, 451, n. 19.

19 Adorno, *Mahler*, 155–56, 85–86, *et passim*.

20 See above, pp. 35–36.

21 In both key and figuration, this ostinato is uncannily like that in the opening of act I in Musorgsky's *Boris Godunov*, where the aged monk Pimen, by the light of a dim lamp in the monastery, is writing the last chapter of his history of Russia (see de La Grange, "Music about Music," 161).

22 Adorno, *Mahler*, 152.

23 See above, p. 62.

24 Adorno, *Mahler*, 152.

25 See above, p. 76.

26 Eveline Nikkels, *"O Mensch! Gib Acht!": Friedrich Nietzsches Bedeutung für Gustav Mahler* (Amsterdam, 1989), 151.

27 E.g., Hermann Danuser, *Gustav Mahler und seine Zeit* (Laaber, 1991), 215–30; cf., however, *HLGF* III: 1132–33.

28 Wenk, "The Composer as Poet in *Das Lied von der Erde*," 36–38.

29 See above, p. 62.

30 Mahler added this passage at a relatively late stage in the composition of the movement, and considerably reworked it before arriving at the version we know; see Hefling, "*Das Lied von der Erde*: Mahler's Symphony for Voices and Orchestra – or Piano," 323–25.

31 Adorno, *Mahler*, 152 (translation modified).

32 Ibid., 145–46; he acknowledges, however, that the two artists knew nothing of each other and probably would not have understood one another.

33 See above, p. 62.

34 See above, p. 76.

35 Cf. the translation in the Appendix, as well as *SSLD*, 271–73 or *HLGF* III: 1148–50.

36 Personal communication, quoted by permission.

37 Hans Swarowsky, *Wahrung der Gestalt* (Vienna, 1979), 126, provides a simplification of bars 90–93 (fig. 15 − 2 ff.) that Mahler supposedly suggested to Sarah Charles Cahier, who subsequently passed it on to Webern ("V" indicates where a breath is to be taken):

hin, ü - ber Blu-men, Grä-ser wan-ken hin die Hü - fe, zer-

stamp - fen jäh im Sturm die hin - ge-sunk'- nen Blü-ten,   wie

38 Adorno, *Mahler*, 145–46, here at 146 (translation modified).

39 See above, p. 33.

40 See above, pp. 63, 75, and 76.

41 Adorno, *Mahler*, 152–53, translation modified.

42 Floros, *Gustav Mahler*, II: 142–43, 311–17, 367–68, and *SSLD*, 475–76.

43 Bekker, *Gustav Mahlers Sinfonien*, 332.

44 See above, pp. 72 and 64.

45 Bethge, *Die chinesische Flöte*, 111, n. to p. 18.

46 Bailey, "*Das Lied von der Erde*: Tonal Language and Formal Design."

47 Performed with Mildred Miller, Ernst Haefliger, and the New York Philharmonic; variously issued on the Columbia, CBS Masterworks, and Sony labels.

48 But see also n. 12 above.

49 See e.g. Antoine Dechevrens, "Etude sur le système musical chinois," esp. 536–47 (with musical examples).

50 Cf. also *SSLD*, 359 ff.

51 See above, p. 72.

52 See above, pp. 19 and 18.

53 For a linear analysis of the passage from **10+5** through **13–2**, see Kofi Agawu, "Prolonged Counterpoint in Mahler," in *Mahler Studies*, ed. Hefling, 242–46.

54 Mahler at one point planned to press the dissynchronization of parts even further than he had at figs. **7–10** (see Hefling, "*Das Lied von der Erde*: Mahler's Symphony for Voices and Orchestra – or Piano," 328–32).

55 For the complete text of the poem and further discussion see *HLG* 1: 826 ff. (*HLGF* I: 1070 ff.).

56 For linear analysis of the orchestral passage from figs. **24** to **27**, see Agawu, "Prolonged Counterpoint in Mahler," 235–41.

57 Goethe, *Faust*, part 2, act V, trans. Philip Wayne (New York, 1959), 270; Nietzsche, *Zarathustra*, pt. 4, "The Drunken Song," sec. 10, trans. Kaufmann, 435.

58 Cf. also *SSLD*, 370–73 and 424–31.

59 Letter to Henry Boys, June 1937, in *Letters from a Life: The Selected Letters and Diaries of Benjamin Britten, 1913–1976*, 2 vols., ed. Donald Mitchell (Berkeley, 1991), I: 493; also in *SSLD*, 339–40.

60 Fechner, *Life After Death*, pp. 23–24 (Ger. repr. edn., pp. 9–10).

61 Ibid., 33–35 (Ger. repr. edn., 16–17).

62 Specht, *Gustav Mahler*, 39.

63 Fechner, *Life After Death*, 66, 25, 63, 65–66 (Ger. repr. edn., 40, 10, 38, 39–40).

64 *SSLD*, 347–48, 409, and 489 n. 126; Hermann Danuser, "Musical Manifestations of the End in Wagner and in Post-Wagnerian *Weltanschauungsmusik*," *19th Century Music* 18 (1994): 81; for Specht's review, see above, p. 76.

65 See above, pp. 17–23.

66 Feder, "Gustav Mahler, Dying" (1978), 145 ff.; Feder, "Mahler, Dying" (1998), 90; and personal communication to the present author.

67 *GMB2*, no. 5 (*GMBE*, no. 2b), 18 June 1879.

68 Edward F. Kravitt, "Mahler's Dirges for His Death: February 24, 1901," *Musical Quarterly* 64 (1978): 335–38.

69 *The Birth of Tragedy*, trans. Kaufman, 131.

Select bibliography

Adler, Guido. See below under Reilly, Edward R.

Adorno, Theodor W. *Mahler: Eine musikalische Physiognomik*. Frankfurt am Main, 1960.

Mahler: A Musical Physiognomy. Translated by Edmund Jephcott. Chicago, 1992.

Quasi una fantasia: Essays on Modern Music. Translated by Rodney Livingstone. London, 1992.

Andraschke, Peter. "Hans Bethge und Gustav Mahler." In *Gustav Mahler: Leben, Werk, Interpretation, Rezeption. Kongreßbericht zum IV. Internationalen Gewandhaus-Symposium anläßlich der Gewandhaus-Festtage 1985*, 95–101. Leipzig, 1990.

Bailey, Robert. "*Das Lied von der Erde*: Tonal Language and Formal Design." Unpublished paper presented to the Forty-Fourth Annual Meeting of the American Musicological Society, Minneapolis, October 1978, and also to the Colorado MahlerFest, Boulder, January 1998.

Bauer-Lechner, Natalie. *Gustav Mahler in den Erinnerungen von Natalie Bauer-Lechner*. Edited by Herbert Killian, with annotations by Knud Martner. Hamburg, 1984. [*NBL2*]

Recollections of Gustav Mahler. Translated by Dika Newlin. Edited by Peter Franklin. Cambridge, 1980. [*NBLE*]

Bekker, Paul. *Gustav Mahlers Sinfonien*. Berlin, 1921. Reprinted, Tutzing, 1969.

Bethge, Eberhard. "Hans Bethge and *Das Lied von der Erde*." Translated by Morten Solvik. *News About Mahler Research* 35 (April 1996): 15–21.

Bethge, Hans. *Die chinesische Flöte: Nachdichtungen chinesischer Lyrik*. Leipzig, 1907. [Variously reprinted.]

Blaukopf, Kurt, ed. and comp. *Mahler: A Documentary Study*. With contributions by Zoltan Roman. Translated by Paul Baker et al. New York, 1976.

Brand, Juliane, Christopher Hailey, and Donald Harris, eds. *The Berg–Schoenberg Correspondence: Selected Letters*. Translated by J. Brand and C. Hailey. New York, 1987.

Brinkmann, Reinhold. "Das ungenaue Unisono: Sechs Kommentare zu Schumanns 'Zwielicht.'" *Musik-Konzepte*, vol. XCV: *Schumann und Eichendorff*,
49–70. Edited by Heinz-Klaus Metzger and Rainer Riehn. Munich, 1997.

Danuser, Hermann. *Gustav Mahler: Das Lied von der Erde*. Meisterwerke der
Musik, vol. XXV. Munich, 1986.

   Gustav Mahler und seine Zeit. Laaber, 1991.

   "Musical Manifestations of the End in Wagner and in Post-Wagnerian Weltanschauungsmusik." *19th Century Music* 18 (1994): 64–82.

Danuser, Hermann, ed. *Gustav Mahler*. Wege der Forschung, vol. 653. Darmstadt, 1992.

de La Grange, Henry-Louis. *Gustav Mahler: Chronique d'une vie*. 3 vols. Paris:
Fayard, 1979–84. [*HLGF*]

   Mahler. Vol. I. Garden City, 1973. [*HLG* 1]

   Gustav Mahler. Vol. II: *Vienna: The Years of Challenge (1897–1904)*. Oxford,
1995. [*HLG* 2]

Fechner, Gustav Theodor. *Das Büchlein vom Leben nach dem Tode*. Dresden,
1836. Reprinted with a preface by Wilhelm Wandt. Leipzig, n.d. Translated by Mary C. Wadsworth as *Life After Death*. New York, 1943.

Feder, Stuart. "Gustav Mahler, Dying." *International Review of Psycho-Analysis*
5 (1978): 125–48.

   "Gustav Mahler um Mitternacht." *International Review of Psycho-Analysis* 7
(1980): 11–25.

   "Mahler, Dying." *Chord and Discord* 3/2 [final issue] (1998): 84–102.

Floros, Constantin. *Gustav Mahler*. 3 vols. Wiesbaden, 1977–85.

   Gustav Mahler: The Symphonies. Translated by Vernon Wicker. Portland,
Oreg., 1993.

   "Weltanschauung und Symphonik bei Mahler." In *Beiträge '79–81 der Öster-
reichischen Gesellschaft für Musik: Gustav Mahler Kolloquium 1979*, 29–39.
Kassel, 1981. Reprinted in *Gustav Mahler*, ed. Hermann Danuser, 344–61.
Wege der Forschung, vol. 653. Darmstadt, 1992.

Franklin, Peter. *Mahler: Symphony No. 3*. Cambridge Music Handbooks. Cambridge, 1991.

Hamao, Fusako. "The Sources of the Texts in Mahler's *Das Lied von der Erde*."
19th Century Music 19 (1995): 83–95.

Hefling, Stephen E. "The Composition of Mahler's 'Ich bin der Welt abhanden
gekommen.'" In *Gustav Mahler*, ed. Hermann Danuser, 96–158. Wege der
Forschung, vol. 653. Darmstadt, 1992.

   "*Das Lied von der Erde*: Mahler's Symphony for Voices and Orchestra – or
Piano." *Journal of Musicology* 10 (1992): 293–340.

"Mahler: Symphonies 1–4." In *The Nineteenth-Century Symphony*, ed. D. Kern Holoman, 369–416. Studies in Musical Genres and Repertoires, R. Larry Todd, general ed. New York, 1997.

"Mahler's 'Todtenfeier' and the Problem of Program Music." *19th Century Music* 12 (1988): 27–53.

Hefling, Stephen E., ed. *Mahler Studies*. Cambridge, 1997.

Johnston, William M. *The Austrian Mind: An Intellectual and Social History, 1848–1938*. Berkeley, 1972.

Lebrecht, Norman. *Mahler Remembered*. New York, 1988.

Lo, Kii-Ming. "Chinesische Dichtung als Text-Grundlage für Mahlers 'Lied von der Erde.'" In *Das Gustav-Mahler-Fest Hamburg 1989: Bericht über den Internationalen Gustav-Mahler-Kongreß*, 509–28. Edited by Matthias Theodor Vogt. Kassel, 1991.

Mahler, Alma. *Gustav Mahler: Erinnerungen und Briefe*. 2nd edn. Amsterdam, 1949.

   Gustav Mahler: Memories and Letters. 4th edn., revised and enlarged by Donald Mitchell and Knud Martner. Translated by Basil Creighton. London, 1990.

Mahler, Gustav. *Adagietto [from the Fifth Symphony]: Facsimile, Documentation, Recording*. Edited by Gilbert E. Kaplan. New York: The Kaplan Foundation, 1992; distributed by Faber Music, London.

   Ein Glück ohne Ruh': Die Briefe Gustav Mahlers an Alma. Edited by Henry-Louis de La Grange and Günther Weiß. Berlin, 1995.

   Gustav Mahler Briefe. Revised and enlarged edition by Herta Blaukopf. Vienna, 1982. [*GMB2*]

   Gustav Mahler – Richard Strauss: Briefwechsel 1888–1911. Edited by Herta Blaukopf. Munich, 1980. Translated by Edmund Jephcott as *Gustav Mahler – Richard Strauss: Correspondence*. Chicago, 1984.

   Gustav Mahler und Holland: Briefe. Edited by Eduard Reeser. Vienna, 1980.

   Sämtliche Werke: Kritische Gesamtausgabe. Edited by the Internationale Gustav Mahler Gesellschaft, Vienna. [Various publishers], 1960– .

   Selected Letters of Gustav Mahler. Edited by Knud Martner. Translated by Eithne Wilkins, Ernst Kaiser, and Bill Hopkins. New York, 1979. [*GMBE*]

   Symphony No. 2 in C minor, "Resurrection": Facsimile. Edited by Gilbert E. Kaplan. New York, 1986.

   Unbekannte Briefe. Edited by Herta Blaukopf et al. Vienna, 1983. Translated by Richart Stokes as *Mahler's Unknown Letters*. London, 1986.

McGrath, William J. *Dionysian Art and Populist Politics in Austria*. New Haven, 1974.

Mitchell, Donald. *Gustav Mahler: The Early Years*. Revised and edited by Paul Banks and David Matthews. Berkeley and Los Angeles, 1980.
Gustav Mahler: The Wunderhorn Years. Boulder, Colo., 1976. Reprinted, Berkeley and Los Angeles, 1980.
Gustav Mahler. Vol. III: *Songs and Symphonies of Life and Death*. Berkeley and Los Angeles, 1985. [*SSLD*]
Mulder, Ernest W. *Gustav Mahler, "Das Lied von der Erde": Een critisch-analytische studie*. Amsterdam, 1951.
Nachrichten zur Mahler-Forschung / News About Mahler Research. Vienna: Internationale Gustav Mahler Gesellschaft, 1976– .
Namenwirth, Simon Michael. *Gustav Mahler: A Critical Bibliography*. 3 vols. Wiesbaden, 1987.
Nietzsche, Friedrich. *The Birth of Tragedy*. Translated by Walter Kaufmann. Vintage Books. New York, 1967.
Thus Spoke Zarathustra. Translated by Walter Kaufmann in *The Portable Nietzsche*. New York, 1968.
Nikkels, Eveline. *"O Mensch! Gib Acht! Friedrich Nietzsches Bedeutung für Gustav Mahler*. Amsterdam, 1989.
Reilly, Edward R. "A Brief History of the Manuscripts." In Mahler, *Symphony No. 2 in C minor, "Resurrection": Facsimile*. Edited by Gilbert E. Kaplan. New York, 1986.
Gustav Mahler and Guido Adler: Records of a Friendship. Cambridge, 1982. [Includes an English translation of Adler's 1916 monograph *Gustav Mahler*.]
"Mahler's Manuscripts and What They Can Tell Us: An Informal Consideration." *Muziek & Wetenschap: Dutch Journal for Musicology* 5/3 (1995–96): 363–83.
Roman, Zoltan. "Aesthetic Symbiosis and Structural Metaphor in Mahler's *Das Lied von der Erde*." In *Festschrift Kurt Blaukopf*. Edited by Irmgard Bontinck and Otto Brusatti. Vienna, 1975.
"Between *Jugendstil* and Expressionism: The Orient as Symbol and Artifice in *Das Lied von der Erde* (Or: 'Warum ist Mahlers Werk so schwer verständlich?')." In International Musicological Society, *Tradition and Its Future in Music: Report of SIMS 1990 Osaka*. Tokyo, 1991.
Gustav Mahler's American Years, 1907–1911. Stuyvesant, NY, 1989.
Schopenhauer, Arthur. *The World as Will and Representation*. 2 vols. Translated by E. F. J. Payne. New York, 1966.
Sedlar, Jean W. *India in the Mind of Germany: Schelling, Schopenhauer, and Their Times*. Washington, D.C., 1982.
Specht, Richard. *Gustav Mahler*. Berlin, 1913.

Vondenhoff, Bruno and Eleonore, comps. *Gustav Mahler Dokumentation: Sammlung Eleonore Vondenhoff.* 2 vols. Publikationen des Instituts für Österreichische Musikdokumentation, ed. Franz Grasberger and Günter Brosche. Tutzing, 1978–83.

Wagner, Richard. "Beethoven [1870]." In *Richard Wagner's Prose Works,* translated by William Ashton Ellis. Vol. V: *Actors and Singers,* 57–126. London, 1896. Reprinted, New York, 1966.

Walter, Bruno. *Gustav Mahler.* Vienna, 1936. English translation by James Galston. New York, 1941. Reprinted, New York, 1973.

Theme and Variations: An Autobiography. New York, 1946.

Wenk, Arthur. "The Composer as Poet in *Das Lied von der Erde.*" *19th Century Music* 1 (1977): 33–47.

Index

Index

CPSIA information can be obtained
at www.ICGtesting.com
Printed in the USA
LVOW03s1955081217
559123LV00003B/264/P

9 780521 475587